Insulin – A Voice for Choice

Acknowledgements

I would like to thank all the following descriptors for their work and their support:

Eva Mathez
Executive Director, Foundation Nutrition and Diabetes, Switzerland

Colleen Fuller
President, PharmaWatch, Canada; co-founder, Canadian Society for Diabetic Rights; health and prescription drug policy researcher and writer

Philip Corfman
Former Director, Center of Population Research, National Institutes of Health, and Reviewing Medical Officer, Food and Drug Administration, USA

Jenny Hirst
Co-Chairman, Insulin Dependent Diabetes Trust, UK

Also, I would like to thank the following collaborators who made this book possible: Nina Bollhalder Sureskumaran, Natalie Escher, Béatrice Fatzer, Bettina Geier, Pia Heiniger, Henriette Ludwig, Irène Michel-Schmid, Prisca Rotzler Köhli, Greta Rye, Bettina Schär, Andrea Sibold, and Claudia Teuscher Möckli.

Finally, I wish to thank Thea Teuscher-Kaiser – my life-long companion – who has lovingly and patiently supported me over the years.

Arthur Teuscher

Insulin – A Voice for Choice

9 figures and 8 tables, 2007

KARGER

Basel · Freiburg · Paris · London · New York ·
Bangalore · Bangkok · Singapore · Tokyo · Sydney

Dr. Arthur Teuscher
Emeritus Professor of Diabetology
University of Bern Medical School
Foundation Nutrition and Diabetes
Beaulieustrasse 88
CH–3012 Bern
Switzerland

Library of Congress Cataloging-in-Publication Data

Teuscher, Arthur.
Insulin : a voice for choice / Arthur Teuscher.
p. ; cm.
Includes bibliographical references and index.
ISBN 978-3-8055-8353-4 (soft cover : alk. paper)
1. Insulin. 2. Insulin–Synthesis. 3. Insulin–Derivatives. 4. Recombinant human insulin. 5. Hypoglycemic agents industry. 6. Diabetes–Chemotherapy–Evaluation. I. Title.
[DNLM: 1. Insulin–Comparative Study. 2. Drug Industry. 3. Hypoglycemia–chemically induced. 4. Hypoglycemic Agents–Comparative Study. WK 820 T351i 2007]
QP572.I5T48 2007
612.3'4–dc22

2007030628

www.karger.com
Printed in Switzerland on acid-free and non-aging paper (ISO 9706) by Reinhardt Druck, Basel
ISBN 978–3–8055–8353–4

Contents

Foreword

On October 29, 1982, the United States Food and Drug Administration (FDA) approved an application by Eli Lilly and Company of Indianapolis, Ind. to market its new synthesized recombinant DNA insulin. The FDA's 4-month review of this first medical product of biotechnology was remarkably less than the average time for drug reviews in those days, suggesting unusual enthusiasm by the FDA staff for the product. The product's name, also subject to FDA approval, was 'Humulin', a name which contradicted the agency's long-standing regulation disallowing '"fanciful" names or false and/or misleading claims embedded in the name' [1].[1]

In fact, and as noted in this remarkable book, Humulin and other synthetic insulins marketed by other companies are by no means identical to natural human insulin as the name, and the marketing, have suggested. Nevertheless, manufacturers re-enforced this misapprehension with a sophisticated and aggressive marketing strategy based, in part, on the premise that 'human' insulin is identical to insulin produced by nondiabetics and therefore must be safer and more effective than insulin obtained from animals. Thousands of physicians, targeted by drug company sales representatives, have internalized that message and have repeated it to their patients.

[1] An example of an intervention by the FDA was its ruling that an oral contraceptive marketed as 'Marvelon' in many countries could not carry this name in the United States since it suggested that the drug was 'marvelous'. Similarly, 'Humulin' suggests that the product is human insulin, a false claim.

It would take a courageous and innovative person to challenge the claims of such a well-financed pharmaceutical marketing strategy. However, as this book demonstrates, Professor Arthur Teuscher was not only well qualified to take on the task but also had the drive and social responsibility to devote an enormous amount of time and energy to this issue. After graduating from the University of Bern Medical School in 1951, he pursued postgraduate studies in endocrinology at the Medical Academy of the Free University of Berlin and the Heinrich-Heine University of Düsseldorf, in nephrology at the University of Bern, and in diabetology at the Joslin Clinic in Boston, Mass. He returned to Bern to specialize in diabetes and other endocrine diseases, becoming one of the first diabetologists in Europe. In 1966 Professor Teuscher established the Diabetes Section at the University of Bern Medical School and in time was appointed Professor of Diabetology. He founded the European Diabetes Epidemiology Group and the European Diabetes and Nutrition Study Group and became a respected member of the World Health Organization's Multinational Study Group on Vascular Diseases in Diabetes.

Like many physicians, Professor Teuscher was influenced by the persistent promotion of 'human' insulin as a significant breakthrough in diabetes treatment. Hoping and expecting to pass the benefits of science and technology to his diabetic patients he suggested that some of them switch to the new product soon after it became available. He did this in good conscience, persuaded, in part, by the scientific enthusiasm worldwide for this first example of the application of recombinant technology to medicine.[2]

As poignantly described in the chapter on Hazards of 'Human' Insulin Hypoglycemia, Professor Teuscher was deeply affected by the death of one of his patients who had chosen to switch to 'human' insulin. Until his death, this 20-year-old man had controlled his diabetes very intelligently. Indeed, he was a pharmacology graduate student and certainly had a good understanding of his disease and insulin treatment. This tragedy motivated Professor Teuscher to begin on his extraordinary and resolute campaign to alert physicians and patients to the potential dangers of synthetic insulin and to his tireless efforts for the continued availability of natural insulin.

His first notable achievement in this endeavor was to co-author, with W.G. Berger, an article in *The Lancet* documenting the case history of this patient and of two others who experienced life-threatening problems with 'human' insulin. The study found that, after a switch from animal to 'human' insulin, hypoglycemia symptoms in all three patients were less pronounced, resulting in diminished

[2] It may be that this enthusiasm accounts for the remarkably rapid approval of the product by the US Food and Drug Administration (FDA) in October 1982.

warnings of impending unconsciousness [2]. The article marked the beginning of a long crusade to develop an evidence-based approach to insulin therapy which underscored the importance of safety and efficacy, as well as patients' quality of life. Soon after Professor Teuscher and Dr. Matthias Egger[3] [3] published a more comprehensive study of the problem in *The Lancet* entitled Human Insulin Hypoglycaemia Unawareness effectively challenging the safety of 'human' insulins in some diabetics. As noted elsewhere in this book, this was followed by a series of scientific articles in other major medical journals which established without doubt that 'human' insulin is indeed less safe than natural insulin in some diabetics.

Professor Teuscher focused much of his efforts on both insulin producers and physicians, but he also did what very few diabetologists had done: he shared his evidence with the emerging movement of diabetic patients fighting for continued access to animal insulin. Despite the acknowledgment by the manufacturers of the potential dangers of 'human' insulin – as evidenced by the boxed drug warning included on all 'human' insulin labels – they promptly started to withdraw natural insulin from markets all over the world in favor of more expensive 'human' brands. As a result, the profits of insulin manufacturers increased significantly, as more affordable animal insulins disappeared from the market in many countries around the world. An unethical and insidious marketing ploy left many local pharmacies without animal insulin, forcing diabetic patients to buy 'human' insulin. This effectively forced a switch, often without the informed consent of the patient, and with little or no information about potential side effects.

It is disturbing to note that market forces have been particularly heavy-handed in developing countries with the result that animal insulin, whether imported or domestically produced, is impossible to obtain in many cases.[4] In response, the persistent and ever-innovative Professor Teuscher extended his reach by bringing animal insulin from India to Dar es Salaam in Tanzania in a remarkable self-sustained program developed with the local City Council Urban Health Project and the Swiss Tropical Institute and supported by the Foundation on Nutrition and Diabetes in Bern.

It is difficult to contest the might of 'Big Pharma', but fortunately advocates of animal insulin are also very much involved, as described by Jenny Hirst in the chapter on Advocacy. Professor Teuscher has earned international respect

[3] Dr Egger is currently Chair, Clinical Reader in Epidemiology and Public Health Medicine, Department of Social Medicine, University of Bristol, UK.

[4] This is also the case in the United States, where pork and beef insulins have been completely withdrawn from the market. However, patients may import small amounts of natural insulin for their personal use.

and admiration within what is now an emerging global movement to support an animal insulin option. Like him, activists are working to ensure that scientific evidence continues to influence the treatment and management of this complex disease. Animal insulin is experiencing a resurgence in the UK and in Canada, and with ongoing efforts at both national and international levels, there is good reason to hope that this will occur in other countries as well.

We are certain that as others join Professor Teuscher and the advocates identified in this book, 'the right of free choice' will be secured, and natural insulin will become available and affordable worldwide for all who need it.

Philip Corfman

References

1 Jenkins JJ: Proprietary Names and the Drug Approval Process. Washington, Center for Drug Evaluation and Research, Office of New Drugs, 2003.

2 Teuscher A, Berger WG: Hypoglycaemia unawareness in diabetics transferred from beef/porcine insulin to human insulin. Lancet 1987;ii:382–385.

3 Teuscher A, Egger M: Human insulin hypoglycaemia unawareness. Lancet 1989;i:1072.

Prologue

Dissimilarity of Natural and Recombinant 'Human' Insulin

Case History of M.B.

This is the unique history of 61-year-old M.B., a Swiss woman with type 1 diabetes, who grew up on a farm in the canton of Bern after World War 2. She developed juvenile diabetes at the age of 5 and presented with unstable diabetes from youth onwards.

From Porcine to 'Human' Insulin with Hypoglycemia Unawareness

In 1987 a diabetologist changed her regimen, replacing porcine with DNA recombinant 'human' fast-acting and isophane insulin. Her diabetes control deteriorated immediately. She had at least one or two unconscious hypoglycemia events per week. Her diabetologist went so far as to suggest that she, being a religious person, should pray and 'leave her life in the hands of God' in order to obtain a more stable diabetes.

Unconscious Hypoglycemia Unawareness in West Africa

M.B. took the doctor's advice seriously and moved to Conakry (Guinea) in 1987 with her husband. They set up a health center and a school in the outskirts of the capital, both of which are still operating. She continued to suffer abrupt hypoglycemia events, without any warning symptoms, 2–3 times a week, occasionally twice a day, and ongoing mental depression. She would drop unexpectedly to the floor. Her husband had to reanimate her with glucose and force her to eat when he came home from work.

'Human' Insulin Was Not the Solution: Returning to Switzerland

M.B. was referred to the diabetes center in Bern by a friend whose diabetic son was back in good health after changing from 'human' back to porcine insulin. He had had several car accidents due to hypoglycemia unawareness while on 'human' insulin, but, once on porcine insulin, he no longer had any accidents, and was able to get his driving license back.

M.B. came under my care in 1995. An African physician had recommended that she returned to Europe because of her continuing unconscious hypoglycemic events, often ending in collapse and sometimes with epileptic seizures.

Going back to 'Friendly' Porcine Insulin

At her first visit, she was on 3–5 units of fast-acting 'human' insulin before meals, 8–10 units of isophane 'human' insulin at breakfast and 2–3 units in the evening. Her HbA1c was 8%. At the first consultation, she was switched to fast-acting and isophane porcine insulins, the same insulin types, with the same doses. She immediately stopped being depressed and emotionally unstable, and she regained the classical hypoglycemia warning symptoms of sweating, tremor, and hunger. This continued to be the case for the next 7 years.

Her blood sugar values were still unstable, but without abrupt hypoglycemia coma. Changing from 10 units of porcine isophane insulin to 3 units of porcine Semilente MC (amorphous zinc suspension) at bedtime prevented postmidnight hypoglycemia. The kinetics and dynamics of porcine insulin Semilente MC in small doses at bedtime (10-12 p.m.) very rarely produce postmidnight hypoglycemia.

A trial for smoother control using an insulin pump was not successful.

Islet Cell Transplantation: Pancreatic Human Insulin Is Not Identical to Recombinant 'Human' Insulin

M.B. was selected as one of the first Swiss candidates for an intrahepatic islet cell transplantation under the *Edmonton Protocol*[5] at the University Hospital of Geneva. The intrahepatic injection of islet cells from two human pancreases was performed in 2002.

For the last 5 years, the patient has had no insulin treatment. She occasionally takes 1 unit of porcine fast-acting insulin 'as a precaution' at her own discretion when her blood sugar is 8 mmol/l after a bit of chocolate. Her HbA1c dropped from 8% before the transplantation to 5.5–5.9% (normal) and has remained at that level for the last 5 years. Islet transplantation resulted in stabilized blood glucose levels of 4–6 mmol/l before breakfast and rarely 7 before the evening meal.

[5] See http://www.islet.ca/.

The main subjective features of a full quality of life have been restored after transplantation: happiness, clear voice, involvement in physical and mental work, disappearance of depression, and the ability to continue with her health project in Guinea. She tolerates immunotherapy well. Laboratory data show absence of diabetes with normal glucose tolerance and no evidence of long-term neurovascular or renal disease.

Conclusion

M.B. is a case of successful islet cell transplantation, but I maintain that in many cases of 'human insulin hypoglycemia unawareness', a transplantation can be prevented by changing from synthetic 'human' to porcine insulin.

In M.B.'s case, full quality of life could only be obtained with islet cell transplantation.

Overview of Insulin Therapy

Definitions

Diabetes and Insulin

Diabetes mellitus is characterized by too much sugar in the blood circulation and extracellular fluids. Indeed, 'mellitus' is derived from the Latin word for honey. The term alludes to the fact that a person with diabetes passes sugar through the urine, thus making it sweet. This phenomenon was the way diabetes was first diagnosed.

With this condition, the body cannot process glucose in the life-sustaining, energy-producing and storage organs. Glucose is derived from the digestion of starch from bread, potatoes, pasta, rice, fruit, products containing sugar, sweet drinks and so on. In addition, the liver and muscles independently produce glucose from stored glycogen (starch) when the blood sugar level decreases or is too low.

Insulin is produced in the islet cells of the pancreas (a gland behind the stomach) of humans and other mammals. This peptide hormone, a small biochemical protein, is responsible for the transfer of blood sugar into the body cells through insulin receptors in the cell walls. Besides producing insulin, the pancreas also produces digestive enzymes such as amylase, peptidase and lipase that break down starches into sugars, proteins into amino acids, and fats into fatty acids.

Since insulin is inactivated by intestinal enzymes and thus cannot be taken by mouth, at present it must be administered by injection to permit its activity. The subcutaneous method is ideal in most circumstances. Insulin is usually injected into the upper quadrants of the abdomen if the insulin is short-acting or into the thighs if the insulin is intermediate or long-acting. Injection into the upper arm may provide faster absorption, especially if the patient exercises following the injection.

Insulin inhalers to absorb insulin through the lungs have been tested successfully and were approved for type 2 diabetes by registration agencies in 2006.

Two Types of Diabetes

Diabetes can have different causes. Most people who have diabetes are type 1 or type 2, less than 5% suffer from other forms of diabetes.

Type 1 diabetes mellitus (T1D), also called insulin-dependent diabetes (IDDM), characteristically develops in children and young people, but may also occur in middle-aged persons and senior citizens. In this type of diabetes, most if not all insulin cells are destroyed, probably immunologically, thus producing a severe insulin deficiency.

Type 1 diabetes requires treatment with insulin injections and an individually adjusted diet and exercise program. Such a diet is not sugar-free but one that is rich in carbohydrates and fibers, with moderate amounts of meat and fat. The major complications of type 1 diabetes are long-term problems with the eyes, nerves, heart, arteries and the kidneys.

Type 2 diabetes (T2D), also known as non-insulin-dependent diabetes (NIDDM), develops if there is peripheral resistance to the action of insulin in the insulin receptors in muscles, the heart, brain and nerve cells, fat, and kidneys. Type 2 diabetes occurs primarily in individuals who are overweight and develops at increasing rates in individuals over the age of 40. Initial treatment may be effective by simply changing the diet and increasing physical activity. In many cases, oral antidiabetic drugs are required, and in about 30–50% of type 2 diabetics insulin may be found to be required as well.

The aim of good blood glucose control is to maintain the blood sugar level at 5–7 mmol/l (90–130 mg/dl) before eating and less than 8–10 mmol/l (140–180 mg/dl) about 1–2 h after food intake. With the administration of oral drugs and, at times, insulin, it is often possible to prevent complications of diabetes, including neurovascular complications and the occurrence of sudden hypoglycemia (blood sugar levels that are too low) as discussed below.

The Regulatory Blood Glucose System

The body has a complicated system of controls to maintain blood glucose levels, by storing glucose as glycogen in the liver, the muscle system and kidneys. The two hormones, insulin and glucagon, produced in two different pancreatic cell clusters, play a key role in maintaining this balance.

If the blood sugar level is too low due to insufficient food intake, physical exercise, a poor diet, the excessive use of oral antidiabetic drugs, or an overdose of injected insulin, the glucose-controlling hormones, glucagon, adrenaline and others, are activated to release glucose from the liver and muscle glycogen system in order to raise the blood sugar back to a normal level of 4–8 mmol/l (70–140 mg/dl).

Endocrine Interactions in Diabetic Patients

Normally insulin and glucagon cooperate so well that the blood glucose level remains essentially stable. Unfortunately, a diabetic is no longer fine-tuned in this way. Insulin injected subcutaneously cannot mimic the swift and gentle effects of insulin produced in nondiabetics and glucagon is not produced on demand in the same way. Indeed, the injection of insulin can easily disturb the body's equilibrium and lead to hypoglycemia.

Hyperglycemia

As noted, hyperglycemia may be caused by insufficient insulin supply or insulin resistance by insulin receptors, causing increases in blood sugar levels to more than 10 mmol/l, and much higher in some cases. As a consequence, in both known and occult diabetics, ketoacidosis may develop. In some cases this may lead to hyperglycemic diabetic coma, with or without ketone bodies detectable as acetone in the blood circulation and urine. The symptoms of such an episode are thirst, passing large amounts of urine, extreme fatigue, increasing sleepiness, rapid weight loss, nausea, vomiting, abdominal pains (appendicitis may be falsely diagnosed but may indeed precede diabetic coma), deep respiration and disturbed consciousness.

Elderly persons may face a special risk since they may underestimate the symptoms, not recognizing them as an incipient diabetic coma. Emergency hospitalization is imperative. Hourly intravenous doses of about 6 units of regular fast-acting insulin can be life saving. Provision of an infusion of several liters of physiological (0.9%) saline solution is most important as well as replacing potassium (K^+) losses. Marked dehydration of the body caused by fever, profuse urination and sweating may also develop into a nonketotic coma with unusually high blood glucose levels. In this situation intravenous electrolyte infusions are essential.

Hypoglycemia

If the blood sugar level falls below 2.5 mmol/l, the autonomous nervous system is activated and stimulates the suprarenal gland to secrete adrenaline, which in turn creates warning signals such as restlessness, sweating, tremors and voracious hunger. At the same time, glucagon causes the liver to release glucose, which increases the blood sugar level. In addition, adrenaline acts as a stimulant for glucose production by catabolizing glycogen depots. Hypoglycemia is the most common adverse event of insulin treatment and can occur with any kind of insulin. Immediate food intake is necessary to prevent the consequences of severe hypoglycemia which include loss of cognitive function, seizures, coma, cerebral infarction and death [1].

Species and Types of Insulin

Insulin plays a key role in the regulation of carbohydrate, fat and protein metabolism. The molecule is a small peptide hormone with a complex three-dimensional structure. The manner in which it is folded appears to affect its function. Three varieties of insulins are used in the modern-day treatment of diabetes: (1) animal insulins, (2) recombinant DNA (so-called 'human') insulins and (3) insulin analogues produced by cloned *Escherichia coli* bacteria or yeast cells.

Animal insulins, 'human' insulins and insulin analogues differ in their amino acid sequence (table 1).

The reader is advised that in this book we present 'human' insulin in quotation marks because the product is not identical to the insulin produced by the human body. The use of the term is no more than a devious albeit effective marketing ploy instituted by insulin producers, which apparently began when the Food and Drug Administration (FDA) approved Lilly's request to name its new insulin 'Humulin' for the US market, an action contrary to the FDA's standing rule not to allow the use of a name which suggests that the drug has unique qualities.

Human Insulin (from Humans)

At present it is possible to transplant live human insulin cells (islets) from deceased nondiabetics intravenously into a type 1 diabetic person's liver in an attempt to stimulate the production of insulin.[1] Living donor islet transplantations are possible but rarely successful [2]. This truly 'human insulin' has a stable structure obtained from living healthy beta cells with the full inventory of amino acids and uniform natural insulin molecules. Unfortunately, as with any other transplants, the patients must take immunosuppressive drug therapy throughout their lives. Transplantation is not a standard therapy for curing diabetes.

Animal Insulins

Animal insulins are natural insulin and are obtained from preferably young cattle and pigs. These extracts from natural pancreases are then highly purified and are thus free from the synthetic recombinant processes used in the production of 'human' insulin. Animal insulins are very similar to human insulin; for instance, bovine (beef) insulin differs in only 3 out of 51 amino acids, porcine (pork) insulin in only 1, from the human product (see table 1). Animal insulins

[1] See Edmonton Protocol, http://www.islet.ca/.

Table 1. Amino acid sequence of different insulins

Human insulin[a]		Pork insulin		Beef insulin		Insulin lispro (analogue)	
A chain	B chain	A chain	B chain	A chain	B chain	A chain	B chain
1 GLY	1 PHE	1 GLY	1 PHE	1 GLY	1 PHE	1 GLY	1 PHE
2 ILE	2 VAL	2 ILE	2 VAL	2 ILE	2 VAL	2 ILE	2 VAL
3 VAL	3 ASN	3 VAL	3 ASN	3 VAL	3 ASN	3 VAL	3 ASN
4 GLU	4 GLN	4 GLU	4 GLN	4 GLU	4 GLN	4 GLU	4 GLN
5 GLN	5 HIS	5 GLN	5 HIS	5 GLN	5 HIS	5 GLN	5 HIS
6 CYS	6 LEU	6 CYS	6 LEU	6 CYS	6 LEU	6 CYS	6 LEU
7 CYS -S-S-	7 CYS	7 CYS -S-S-	7 CYS	7 CYS -S-S-	7 CYS	7 CYS -S-S-	7 CYS
8 THR	8 GLY	8 THR	8 GLY	**8 ALA**	8 GLY	8 THR	8 GLY
9 SER	9 SER	9 SER	9 SER	9 SER	9 SER	9 SER	9 SER
10 ILE	10 HIS	10 ILE	10 HIS	**10 VAL**	10 HIS	10 ILE	10 HIS
11 CYS	11 LEU	11 CYS	11 LEU	11 CYS	11 LEU	11 CYS	11 LEU
12 SER	12 VAL	12 SER	12 VAL	12 SER	12 VAL	12 SER	12 VAL
13 LEU	13 GLU	13 LEU	13 GLU	13 LEU	13 GLU	13 LEU	13 GLU
14 TYR	14 ALA	14 TYR	14 ALA	14 TYR	14 ALA	14 TYR	14 ALA
15 GLN	15 LEU	15 GLN	15 LEU	15 GLN	15 LEU	15 GLN	15 LEU
16 LEU	16 TYR	16 LEU	16 TYR	16 LEU	16 TYR	16 LEU	16 TYR
17 GLU	17 LEU	17 GLU	17 LEU	17 GLU	17 LEU	17 GLU	17 LEU
18 ASN	18 VAL	18 ASN	18 VAL	18 ASN	18 VAL	18 ASN	18 VAL
19 TYR	S- 19 CYS	19 TYR	S- 19 CYS	19 TYR	S- 19 CYS	19 TYR	S- 19 CYS
20 CYS -S	20 GLY	20 CYS -S	20 GLY	20 CYS -S	20 GLY	20 CYS -S	20 GLY
21 ASN	21 GLU	21 ASN	21 GLU	21 ASN	21 GLU	21 ASN	21 GLU
	22 ARG		22 ARG		22 ARG		22 ARG
	23 GLY		23 GLY		23 GLY		23 GLY
	24 PHE		24 PHE		24 PHE		24 PHE
	25 PHE		25 PHE		25 PHE		25 PHE
	26 TYR		26 TYR		26 TYR		26 TYR
	27 THR		27 THR		27 THR		27 THR
	28 PRO		28 PRO		28 PRO		**28 LYS**
	29 LYS		29 LYS		29 LYS		**29 PRO**
	30 THR		**30 ALA**		**30 ALA**		30 THR

S–S = Sulfur bridges.

[a] The amino acid sequence of insulin produced by humans and 'human' insulin produced by recombinant DNA technology is the same.

are peptides (small proteins) produced by living pancreatic (beta) cells and are structured as a specific three-dimensional hormone, as is natural human insulin. Animal insulins from beef, pork and whales (whale insulin was produced in the 1920s to overcome the shortage of beef insulin) have been on the market since 1922. Since 1973 they have been as pure as synthetic insulins, so the fear of immunogenic reactions is not justified. Beef insulin is now less commonly used in industrialized countries because of the perceived risk of BSE prion contamination, even though such contamination has never been linked to insulin.

Recombinant Insulin (Also Called 'Human' Insulin)

The term 'human' insulin is misleading. It is not a natural human product but is produced by genetically modified *E. coli* bacteria or yeast cells with the human insulin gene spliced into their genome. Such synthetic insulin may have the peptide structure of truly human insulin, but it is produced artificially under laboratory conditions, outside human pancreatic beta cells. The amino acids are lined up in two different chains of amino acids, produced by two different cloned *E. coli* bacteria or yeast cells. These synthetic products have to be restructured in the laboratory with two sulfur bridges. They are quite different from the organic product which develops in accordance with a natural growth plan.

The first 'human' insulin registered for medical use was produced via recombinant DNA technology with cloned *E. coli* bacteria by Lilly USA in 1982. A different technique was applied to produce 'semisynthetic' 'human' insulin from porcine insulin by cutting off the amino acid alanine B30 and replacing it with threonine (Novo Industrie AS, Hoechst, 1982). Preparations of human sequence insulin should theoretically be less immunogenic, but no real advantage has been shown in clinical trials [3].

Insulin Analogues

Insulin analogues are the third insulin-like species. Starting from recombinant 'human' insulin, their amino acid chain is changed, mainly by exchanging or substituting different amino acids in so-called 'irrelevant' sequences of the molecule. In its molecular structure, an analogue is no longer identical to natural human insulin.

Humalog (insulin lispro), which has been in use since 1996, is an example of an insulin analogue. Because it is a 'monomer' (only one molecule), it is absorbed more quickly into the capillaries and the circulating blood from the subcutaneous fat. Natural insulin on the other hand is produced in pairs of two (dimers) or even six molecules (hexamers). The disadvantage of Humalog is that its kinetics (2–4 h) does not cover the time between two meals adequately. Today, several new genetically engineered insulin analogues are on the market and are advertised as the most advanced therapy for the treatment of diabetes, but this alleged advantage has not yet been demonstrated.

Table 2. Kinetics of insulins

Type of insulin, product	Characteristics	Insulin kinetics (begin and maximal duration of effect) h
Regular	short-acting	½–8
Zinc semilente	intermediate-acting	1½–16
NPH isophane	long-acting	1½–24
Biphasic (example 30/70)	30% regular, 70% isophane	½–24

Table 3. Four insulin activity periods

Time	Insulin sensitivity	Tendency to hypoglycemia
Morning 6–12 a.m.	reduced	high before lunch
Afternoon 12–6 p.m.	increased	high before supper
Evening 6–12 p.m.	low	low
After midnight 12 p.m. to 6 a.m.	high	high, very high around 2 a.m.

Clinical Insulin Review: Pharmacokinetics

There are three popular types of insulin classified according to their duration (kinetics) and peak action (dynamics): short, intermediate and long acting (table 2).

Long-acting bovine and, especially, porcine insulins have been popular for 50 years. Their advantages have been:

- Low hypoglycemia rates compared with 'human' insulin.
- Often only one daily injection is required for 24 h of activity.
- They are useful for diabetics who have difficulty with home glucose monitoring.

It is very important to understand the personal kinetics and dynamics of short-, intermediate- and long-acting insulin in a given diabetic individual. For practical reasons, it is best to monitor kinetics and dynamics in 6-hour periods: morning (6–12 a.m.), afternoon (12–6 p.m.), evening (6–12 p.m.), after midnight (12–6 a.m.). The diurnal concentration of regulatory blood glucose hormones varies from high in the morning to low after midnight. When the level is low, sensitivity to insulin is at its highest and so is the hypoglycemia risk (table 3).

Intensive Insulin Therapy

In 1976, the American Diabetes Association (ADA) advocated intensive insulin therapy to prevent long-term neurological and microvascular complications [4]. This tighter regiment requires the use of insulin with shorter kinetics, thus making more blood glucose tests necessary, more insulin injections, and, in some cases, the use of an insulin pump. The goal is to keep the blood glucose level lower. However hypoglycemia is much more likely to occur with this regimen [5].

Insulin Pumps

Insulin pumps provide subcutaneous insulin infusion according to a timed program and additionally if required to cover meals. They contain short-acting insulin or insulin analogue. During the last decade, pumps have been fairly widely used in developed countries, mainly for 'brittle' type 1 diabetics who cannot achieve smooth control otherwise. They have also been used in diabetic women before and during pregnancy when the control of diabetes can be particularly difficult. It has been shown that the use of insulin pumps in specialized centers does significantly improve diabetes control as measured by HbA1c, although the improvement may be relatively small when compared to good control on intensified treatment with multiple subcutaneous injections. The occurrence of severe hypoglycemic episodes may also decrease with the use of the pump [6].

Unfortunately high financial costs prevent the use of the insulin pump as a large-scale treatment but the reduced number of hospital admissions due to diabetic ketoacidosis, fewer episodes of severe hypoglycemia, and the reduction of late diabetes complications argue effectively for its broader use. There are also attempts to develop a closed-loop pump, also called an 'artificial pancreas', that measures glucose levels, calculates and releases the needed insulin on its own [7].

Insulin Powder to Inhale

Insulin producers have tried for a long time to develop alternatives to the subcutaneous injection. Tests with administration through the skin with patches or with capsules that would not decompose in the stomach have so far been unsuccessful.

A group of pharmaceutical companies has now obtained approval in the US and Europe for an insulin powder that can be inhaled. The preparation, which is marketed under the name 'Exubera', is a short-acting 'human' insulin. Type 1 diabetics who want to use Exubera will still have to use a syringe for the administration of basal insulin. There is no long-term experience with inhaled insulin. This is particularly important because the administered insulin doses are much higher than those required when the insulin is injected.

References

1 World Health Organization: WHO Model Formulary 2002, p 319.

2 Matsumoto S, Okitsu T, Iwanaga Y, Noguchi H, Nagata H, Yonekawa Y, Yamada Y, Fukuda K, Tsukiyama K, Suzuki H, Kawasaki Y, Shimodaira M, Matsuoka K, Shibata T, Kasai Y, Maekawa T, Shapiro J, Tanaka K: Insulin independence after living-donor distal pancreatectomy and islet allotransplantation. Lancet 2005;365:1642–1644.

3 Richter B, Neises G: 'Human' insulin versus animal insulin in people with diabetes mellitus. Cochrane Database Syst Rev 2005;1:CD003816. DOI: 10.1002/14651858.CD003816.pub2.

4 Cahill GF Jr, Etzwiler LD, Freinkel N: 'Control' and diabetes. N Engl J Med 1976;294:1004–1005.

5 DCCT, quoted in http://www.fmcsa.dot.gov/Pdfs/insulin4.pdf, p. 4–12 6.3.2007.

6 Pickup J, Mattock M, Kerry S: Glycaemic control with continuous subcutaneous insulin infusion compared with intensive insulin injections in patients with type 1 diabetes: meta-analysis of randomised controlled trials. BMJ 2002;324:705.

7 Pickup J: How good is glycaemic control during CSII? Do we still need an artificial pancreas? Infusystems Int 2006;5:4.

The History of Insulin

Discovery of Insulin

In 1921 the Canadian scientists Fredrick G. Banting, Charles H. Best, J.J.R. Macleod and James B. Collip discovered insulin, a peptide (small protein hormone) which lowers blood sugar. They extracted insulin from the islets of animal pancreases. Up to that time type 1 diabetes was a virtual death sentence for patients suffering from it. Now, it could for the first time be treated successfully. The researchers gave the patent rights to the University of Toronto so that diabetics worldwide could, through insulin, survive. The scientists refused financial gain in order to serve science, research and humankind – and to conquer diabetes.

First Diabetics on Insulin

A year later, in January 1922, bovine insulin was first given to humans by injection. It was still so impure that as a result of the first insulin injection Leonard Thompson had a 7.5 cm callus at the injection site on his left buttock. The co-discoverers, in particular James Collip, continued their work to purify the insulin extract to make it safer and more effective. Nevertheless, the quality of the insulin administered at that time was far from the quality of today's products. Each vial of insulin had a different effect because of differing purity. That is why Elizabeth Hughes, one of the first diabetics to be treated with insulin, often had hypoglycemic reactions. She also suffered pain and swelling at the injection site, especially when large quantities of insulin were injected [1].

Evolution of Insulins

Animal Insulin

Beginning in 1922, and in the face of great demand for the new medicine, several companies were granted licenses by the University of Toronto to manufacture insulin. In 1936, protamine, a low-weight protein, was used to develop a

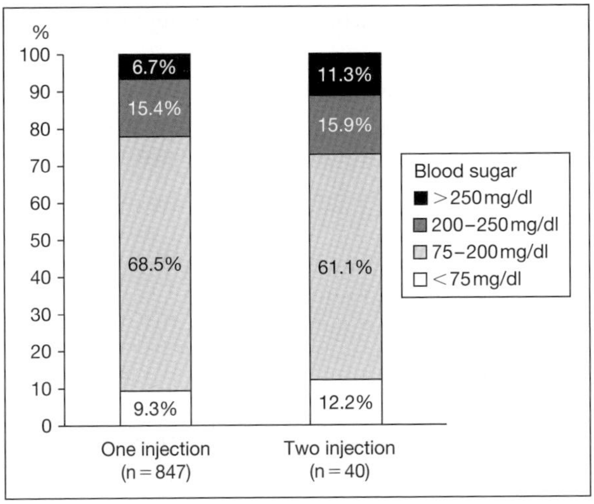

Fig. 1. Percentage distribution of blood sugar levels in 887 cases with insulin zinc suspension (IZS) that were controlled during 1 week of hospitalization [2]. Reprinted with permission from Elsevier.

slow-release insulin. With the availability of protamine, as well as zinc, the first slow-acting insulin was produced. Protamine zinc insulin (PZI) was an insulin whose effect lasted for 24–36 h.

In 1950 yet another approach led to the presently available isophane NPH (neutral protamine Hagedorn) insulin, which is also bound to protamine. It has a maximal effect of 24 h and can be mixed with any proportion of fast-acting regular insulin.

In 1951 the amorphous 'lente' insulins (IZS) – semilente, lente and ultra-lente – were developed. Depending on the proportion of zinc – a natural component of the body's insulin – used, variable kinetic and dynamic effects were obtained without the use of protamine. In a study conducted by Jersild [2], 1,000 patients with type 1 diabetes were switched from NPH isophane to lente and semilente, and of these, 936 patients were controlled satisfactorily with a single morning dose. The other patients needed an additional split dose with a second injection in the evening. Figure 1 shows the patients that were controlled in hospital, where blood glucose monitoring was available: 847 needed 1 injection and 40 needed 2 injections.

Using the same products, Spencer and Morgans [3] got similarly satisfactory results in 83% of 200 patients. Severe hypoglycemia in both studies was rare.

In 1956, the first antidiabetic oral drugs – sulfonamide (tolbutamide, carbutamide) and biguanide derivatives (metformin, phenformin) – came on the market. Before the development of these new drugs, the only drug available for type 2 diabetics was insulin.

In 1974, chromatographic purification techniques allowed the production of highly purified animal insulin (less than 1 pmol/l of protein impurities). This product was called 'monocomponent MC' by Novo and 'single peak' insulin by Eli Lilly. Before this development, porcine and bovine insulin at times caused antibody allergies and lipoatrophy [4]. Today, however, there are no significant differences between the purity of animal and 'human' insulins. Indeed, insulin antibodies are formed at a very low level with both types [5, 6].

'Human' Insulin and Analogues

After several years of laboratory work during the years 1963–1966 human insulin was chemically synthesized in Germany by Meienhofer et al. [7], in China by Kung et al. [8] and in the United States by Katsoyannis et al. [9]. This work demonstrated that human insulin (and other proteins as well) could indeed be synthesized.

In 1975, fully synthetic insulin (CGP 12 831) was synthesized in the laboratories of Ciba-Geigy in Basel. In a clinical trial, 6 patients with diabetes were treated with this insulin for up to 2 weeks [10]. It was not noted in the article that 2 patients experienced more sudden hypoglycemic events than with animal insulin, but apart from that, the synthetic insulin was well tolerated. Charles H. Best, one of the discoverers of insulin, personally commented this step in the evolution of insulin:

'Dear Dr. Teuscher – I have received your letter and the enclosures. … I congratulate your group on the first clinical use of synthetic human insulin. With regards, sincerely – Charles H. Best' [personal letter, July 4th 1977]. For economic reasons, however, large-scale production and subsequent marketing were not undertaken.

In 1978, scientists from the biotechnology corporation Genentech in San Francisco, Calif., using a genetically manipulated plasmid of *E. coli* bacteria, succeeded in producing insulin with the same amino sequence as seen in humans.

In 1980, recombinant DNA 'human' insulin was first tested on 17 nondiabetic volunteers in England. The investigators concluded that 'human' insulin may be slightly more potent than porcine insulin at the low dose, and slightly less so at higher doses. They demanded 'further and continuous careful observation of unexpected side effects' [11]. The study predicted the problems with hypoglycemia unawareness seen later and which are discussed in the next chapter.

The race to mass produce 'human' insulin using gene technology was won by Eli Lilly in 1982 when the FDA approved Humulin R (rapid) and Humulin N (NPH) for the US market. This was followed by Novo's semisynthetic insulins

Actrapid HM and Monotard HM. Eli Lilly and Novo both claimed that these products were identical to actual human insulin, and therefore were the best form of insulin therapy possible.

Since 1996, different insulin analogues have been introduced worldwide. These are characterized by various pharmacokinetics. Today, Humalog (Lilly), Lantus and Apidra (Aventis), Levemir and NovoRapid (Novo Nordisk) are available. A large number of additional analogue insulin formulas are currently being tested.

References

1 Bliss M: The Discovery of Insulin. Chicago, University of Chicago Press, 1982, p 155.
2 Jersild M: Insulin zinc suspension; four years' experience. Lancet 1956;271:1009–1013.
3 Spencer AG, Morgans ME: Lente insulin; four years' experience. Lancet 1956;271:1013–1017.
4 Teuscher A: Treatment of insulin lipoatrophy with monocomponent insulin. Diabetologia 1974;10:211–214.
5 Ho LT, Lam HC, Wu MS, Kwok CF, Jap TS, Tang KT, Wang LM, Liu YF: A twelve month double-blind randomized study of the efficacy and immunogenicity of human and porcine insulins in non-insulin-dependent diabetics. Zhonghua Yi Xue Za Zhi (Taipei) 1991;47:313–319.
6 Balsells M, Corcoy R, Mauricio D, Morales J, Garcia-Patterson A, Carreras G, Puig-Domingo M, de Leiva A: Insulin antibody response to a short course of human insulin therapy in women with gestational diabetes. Diabetes Care 1997;20:1172–1175.
7 Meienhofer J, Schnabel E, Bremer H, et al: Synthese der Insulinketten und ihre Kombination zu insulactiven Präparaten. Z Naturforsch 1963;18:1120.
8 Kung YT, Da YC, Huang WT, et al: Total synthesis of crystalline insulin. Sci Sin 1966;15:544.
9 Katsoyannis PG, Tometsko A, Zalut C: Insulin peptides XII. Human insulin generation by combination of synthetic A and B chains. J Am Chem Soc 1966;88:186.
10 Teuscher A: The biological effect of purely synthetic human insulin in patients with diabetes mellitus. Schweiz Med Wochenschr 1979;109:743–747.
11 Keen H, Glynne A, Pickup JC, et al: Human insulin produced by recombinant DNA technology: safety and hypoglycaemic potency in healthy men. Lancet 1980;ii:398–401.

Insulin Hypoglycemia

Blood Sugar Levels

Hypoglycemia reflects a blood sugar level that is below normal. No matter how carefully patients observe their diabetes, they may not be able to prevent hypoglycemia in every situation. Usually it is easy for the patient to recognize it and to react before a dangerous fall occurs. Every insulin-treated diabetic should know his/her typical warning signs or symptoms and should act early to correct them before a more severe drop in blood sugar occurs. However, even with rigorous monitoring it is not always easy for patients to recognize the warning signs. Indeed, sudden hypoglycemia accompanied by unconsciousness may at times occur without any warning, particularly, as noted below, with the use of 'human' insulins.

Some warning signs, such as behavioral changes, may be recognized by family, friends and colleagues at work. At times, however, help may be refused by the diabetic, who cannot recognize the seriousness of the situation.

Although blood glucose home monitoring devices that enable diabetics to monitor and manage their blood sugar levels have been available since the 1980s sudden hypoglycemia remains a threatening event. Table 4 lists the blood sugar thresholds every diabetic should be familiar with.

Hypoglycemia in People without Insulin Treatment

As noted, hypoglycemia is a frequent adverse event in type 1 diabetics using insulin, but it can also occur in type 2 diabetics who do not use insulin and even in people who do not have diabetes. Some instances where such events may occur are described below.

Hypoglycemia from Antidiabetic Oral Drugs

Approximately 90% of all diabetics have type 2 diabetes and many of them are given oral antidiabetic drugs. Some of these drugs stimulate human pancreatic insulin secretion and others increase sensitivity to insulin. With potent insulin releasers such as sulfonylureas, patients may experience hypoglycemic

Table 4. Interpretation of blood sugar levels

	Blood sugar level	
	mmol/l	mg/dl
Too low ('hypo')	<2.5	<45
Low	2.5	45
Borderline	3–4	54–72
Normal before meals	5–7	90–125
Acceptable after meals	8–10	140–180
Elevated ('hyper')	>10	>180

events produced by the body's own insulin if they are given doses that are too high.

After the introduction in 1970 of glibenclamide, a potent insulin releaser, an epidemic of sudden hypoglycemia-related deaths occurred in elderly diabetics. Their own pancreases were stimulated to produce too much insulin, creating the same abrupt adverse hypoglycemic events seen with 'human' insulin.

Hypoglycemia in Nondiabetics

Nondiabetics can experience what is called reactive hypoglycemia when, in response to the intake of a relatively large amount of carbohydrate, their body releases more insulin than is required. They can prevent such episodes by eating fiber-rich food which causes blood sugar to increase more slowly. Such postprandial hypoglycemic reactions are not unusual after an early breakfast, which normally increases insulin secretion. The blood sugar may fall significantly after about 2 h and people will feel fit again with a second breakfast.

Heavy physical exercise, such as long distance running, may also induce hypoglycemia. Glucose tablets, fruit juices or cola (not the diet variety) can immediately increase the blood sugar level. In everyday life, healthy people may prevent hypoglycemia with snacks between meals.

Insulinoma: An Insulin-Producing Tumor

Occasionally an oversupply of intrinsic insulin may come from beta-cell tumors, called insulinomas, in the pancreas gland. Blood glucose values of less than 2.5 mmol/l (45 mg/dl) and even much lower may be experienced in these rare cases. In such cases, the tumor must be removed, in part because of its often malignant or precancerous nature. The remarkably severe hypoglycemic symptoms seen with insulinomas are similar to those seen with 'human' insulin and may include depression, erratic movements, confusion and aggression.

Signs and Symptoms of Hypoglycemia [1–3]

The first warnings of hypoglycemia occur at a blood sugar level of around 3 mol/l. These autonomous symptoms include:

- Sweating
- Tremor
- Hunger
- Palpitations
- Anxiety
- Shivering
- Sense of warmth

At a blood sugar level of around 2 mmol/l or lower, the neuroglycopenic hypoglycemic symptoms may be more prominent:

- Inability to concentrate
- Confusion
- Dizziness
- Difficulty speaking
- Drowsiness

Other signals of acute hypoglycemia are:

- Nausea
- Tingling around lips
- Weakness
- Blurred vision
- Impaired cognitive function
- Depression
- Behavioral changes and irrational behavior, including aggressiveness, unmotivated laughing, stammered articulation, yawning, becoming silent, absent, erratic car driving
- Fainting
- Unconsciousness
- Seizures/convulsions

From a clinical point of view, 'autonomous', adrenaline-type warnings occur first – at blood sugar levels of around 3 mmol/l whereas 'neuroglycopenic' (brain) symptoms occur later – at blood sugar levels of around 2 mmol/l (fig. 2).

Management of Hypoglycemia

It is very important that insulin-induced hypoglycemia is treated as soon as symptoms occur. Although there are no approved standards to grade

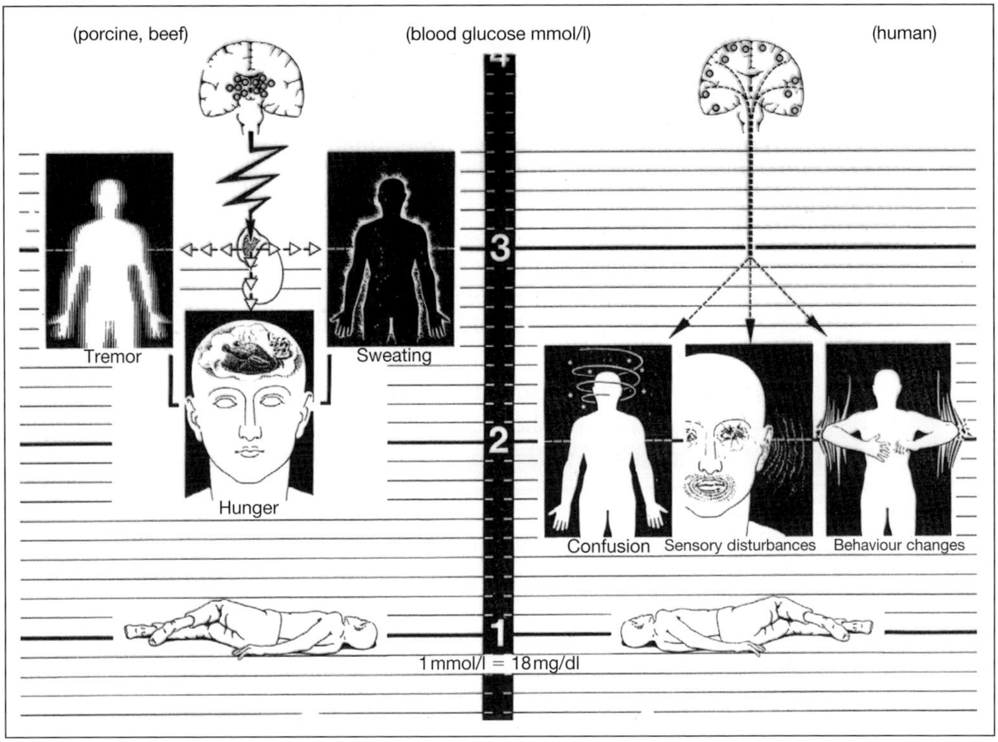

Fig. 2. Symptoms of hypoglycemia with animal (left) and 'human' (right) insulin are illustrated. This figure was drawn to explain the different symptoms to patients. Drawn by Christian Götz, 1988.

hypoglycemia severity, it can be classified roughly into three levels as shown in table 5.

Grade 1: Mild Hypoglycemia

When blood glucose levels are as low as 3–4 mmol/l, the body's adrenaline is stimulated and should elicit the early adrenal warning symptoms, but the classic symptoms of sweating, trembling, palpitations and hunger may not be apparent in some patients, especially in those on 'human' insulin [4, 5].

At times of stress – e.g. while driving a car or working at a machine – low blood sugar should be corrected even if the signs appear to be minimal. At these times, patients should take sugar immediately in forms such as:

- Glucose tablets, 3 or more tablets, one at a time
- Sugar cubes: 2–3 cubes or more
- Sweet drinks containing sugar, such as orange juice or cola (3 dl = 30 g of sugar). 'Light' or 'diet' drinks contain no sugar

Table 5. Levels of hypoglycemia

Grade 1, 'mild'	no outside help required
Grade 2, 'moderately severe'	semiconscious, may need assistance
Grade 3, 'severe'	unconscious, needs outside intervention

This treatment should be repeated several times in ongoing hypoglycemia cases until blood glucose is restored, as determined by symptoms or a blood glucose measurement.

Every diabetic on insulin and/or oral antidiabetic drugs should carry sugar or glucose tablets so he or she can react immediately. While driving, sugar should be easily available, for instance in the pocket of the driver's door.

Grade 2: Moderate Hypoglycemia

In more serious hypoglycemic events, the same warning signals described above may develop, but the brain signals dominate. This condition can also be treated orally with sugar but assistance is often necessary because patients are confused or their cognitive abilities are impaired. After such events it is advisable for the patient to consume snacks such as bread, biscuits or fruit in order to keep the blood sugar within a normal range. Mild or moderate hypoglycemia may develop into severe cases if not treated quickly.

Grade 3: Severe Hypoglycemia

Severe hypoglycemia always requires outside help. The patient may be unconscious and needs emergency services. At home it is important to keep an emergency glucagon injection kit available and this must be stored at 2–8°C (34–44°F). Glucagon may be injected subcutaneously, intramuscularly, or intravenously. The goal is to achieve a blood sugar increase within 5–15 min. Then it is important to provide light food by mouth. Injecting glucagon is in principle a physician's responsibility but in an emergency family members, friends or co-workers may provide the treatment needed. Before glucagon was available, a subcutaneous injection of 1 ml of adrenaline was often effective.

Unconscious people may aspirate liquids and therefore should not be given food or drinks. However, if there appears to be no other way to treat the patient, it may help to place glucose tablets, sugar lumps, honey or jam into the cheek pouch because the swallowing reflexes may still be present.

The History of Insulin Hypoglycemia

Dr. Elliott P. Joslin of Boston, Mass., the director of the first clinic devoted exclusively to diabetes, described the symptoms of hypoglycemia in the 1950s as follows:

'What is an insulin reaction? If too much insulin is given, the blood sugar falls below normal and a "reaction" occurs. The symptoms of a reaction are hunger, tremor, sweating, unconsciousness. Other symptoms are weakness, pallor, faintness, nervousness, dizziness, dilated pupils, double vision, emotional upsets. Nausea and headache are apt to occur if the reaction is due to protamine insulin. A reaction caused by any kind of insulin may progress to unconsciousness and convulsions' [6].

Joslin [7] suggested that when patients thought they might feel a reaction coming, homemade orange juice would be the perfect prevention. The time needed to peel the orange could be used to think about whether the sugar it contained was really needed. This casual approach suggests that the hypoglycemic reactions seen in those days were not as abrupt as the reactions often seen today with 'human' insulin.

An insulin reaction may assume a progressive pattern of physiological responses which begin with certain early warning signs and end in profound coma or convulsions. Tachycardia (rapid heart beat), excessive perspiration, and a sense of anxiety are among the typical early warning signs. It is believed that these symptoms are due to generalized discharge from the sympathetic nervous system. It is usually this sympathetic nervous system hyperactivity which alerts a diabetic to hypoglycemia [8].

T.L., Secretary

The secretary of a church association, who had a 15-year history of unstable diabetes, stated [personal communication]:

'When I feel hypoglycemia coming at lunchtime, I get up, put my jacket on, cross the street, get into the restaurant, order and eat. After a little while I get my hypoglycemia under control. When I was on "human" insulin, I wanted to grab the sugar on the desk but I could not move my arm in that direction. Eventually, my hand grabbed the sugar and I tried to put it in my mouth because of my voracious hunger. "Human" insulin is sharp'.

By 'sharp' the patient appeared to be saying that 'human' insulin acted too aggressively and consequently, as will be shown in the next chapter, she detected a serious problem. Over the last 20 years, the author has collected more than 300 similar cases of sudden hypoglycemia experienced with 'human' insulin. A few of these cases are highlighted in this book.

Nocturnal Hypoglycemia

Fifty to seventy percent of severe hypoglycemic episodes occur during sleep. All people, especially children, are justifiably frightened of the prospect of nighttime hypoglycemia. The greatest risk occurs at around 2 a.m. Intermediate-acting insulins, when injected before the evening meal, reach their peak activity between 1 and 4 a.m., when the body is most sensitive to insulin.

The first 'human' insulin introduced to the market was NPH, an intermediate-acting insulin. Humulin N or Insulatard HM was often given at supper time, eliciting abrupt hypoglycemia soon after midnight, followed by elevated fasting blood sugars in the morning because of its shorter duration and earlier peak. The major problem with nocturnal hypoglycemia is its occurrence during deep sleep, when it may not be noticed soon enough. In such instances, severe reactions may last for several hours until the early morning when the patient wakes up. Even death may occur, as described in the chapter on Hazards of 'Human' Insulin Hypoglycemia.

When unusual restlessness during sleep is noticed by the diabetic's partner or other members of the family it should alarm them. Patients waking up with severe hypoglycemia may be aggressive and reject help, at times causing family disagreements, trauma and/or disruption.

Patients who experience frequent nocturnal hypoglycemia may improve the situation by using a long-acting insulin at bedtime and by reducing the dose given previously before supper by 30–50%. They should take short-acting insulin before supper. If the blood sugar is 10–15 mmol/l or higher at bedtime, 1–3 units of short-acting insulin may be used without increasing the dose of the longer-acting basal insulin. Patients are better able to prevent early morning hypoglycemia if their blood glucose is stabilized above a minimum of 4 mmol/l at 2 a.m.

If the early morning blood sugar is elevated, the late night dose should be increased cautiously, and only after ensuring that the elevation is not due to the counterregulatory effect of too much bedtime insulin. If the bedtime dose is too high it may be reduced carefully. The dose should not be based on the actual blood sugar at the time of injection, but on an early morning blood sugar target of between 5 and 7 mmol/l.

Experience has shown that the best practice is to keep the bedtime dose as low and stable as possible. This should result in satisfactory fasting glucose values and enable a smooth blood sugar profile the following day.

Hypoglycemia after midnight:

- Up to 70% of serious hypoglycemic events occur after midnight during sleep.

- These events may last for several hours.
- The timing of the lowest blood sugar depends on the action profile of the insulin: 'human' insulin peaks earlier than animal insulin, which has slower kinetics.
- If the evening injection is given before supper, the peak activity occurs after midnight when the body is most sensitive to insulin, thereby increasing the risk of hypoglycemia at that time. The long-acting insulin injection should, therefore, be changed from before supper to bedtime and the dose should be reduced by at least 30–50%.
- A bedtime snack is recommended when the blood sugar is low to normal or 1–3 units of rapid-acting insulin may be required when the bedtime blood sugar is elevated.

Semilente Porcine Insulin

Semilente MC porcine insulin, which has been on the market for 50 years, is the best 'good night insulin' for a large number of people. The intermediate bedtime dose is 30–50% less than that required by patients using isophane NPH insulin. Semilente has an intermediate activity after midnight and increased dynamics at around 4 a.m., when endogenous liver glucose production increases the blood sugar level.

Semilente insulin is still available in some European countries. It was originally produced by Novo Nordisk Denmark, which discontinued marketing this type of insulin after May 1, 2007. Suppliers in Eastern Europe still produce this useful product and it may be imported by some pharmacies. At the time Novo Nordisk announced the withdrawal of Semilente MC, at least 12,000 patients in Germany were treated with this insulin, among them many children and teenagers [9].

Unfortunately, there is no 'human' or analogue insulin with the same kinetics as semilente insulin, the best insulin for preventing nighttime hypoglycemia and achieving acceptable fasting blood sugar levels the following morning.

In 1997, a double-blind Novo Nordisk study conducted in 15 European centers compared porcine Semilente MC with the 'human' product, Monotard HM. Among the 117 subjects with type 1 diabetes significantly lower fasting blood sugar levels before breakfast and more stable glucose control were achieved by those using Semilente MC.[2] Novo Nordisk did not publish

[2] Renner R, Berger W, Hirschberger S, Kuglin B, Pramming S: Metabolische Kontrolle während der Nacht bei Typ I Diabetikern: Insulin Semilente MC versus Monotard HM. Poster presentation by Novo Nordisk, 1997.

Table 6. Number and grade of nocturnal hypoglycemic episodes as perceived by the patient on different insulins[2]

Grade of hypoglycemia	NPH	Semilente
No problem	–	13
Mild	11	34
Moderately severe	22	0
Severe	18	4

the details of the study, perhaps because it was promoting its new product, Monotard HM.

The advantages of Semilente MC were again confirmed during a study in which we changed the therapy of 51 type 1 diabetic patients from porcine NPH to semilente insulin at bedtime.[3] All patients had previously reported at least 1 serious nocturnal hypoglycemic episode. As shown in table 6, bedtime semilente was significantly less likely to induce serious nocturnal hypoglycemia than NPH insulin, at smaller insulin doses and with better HbA1c results.

A double-blind crossover study by Strasser et al. [10] in 1993 looked at whether semilente insulin could be used to control fasting hyperglycemia in type 1 diabetic patients. Three doses of regular insulin were given before the meals and NPH insulin and semilente at 10:00p.m. Nighttime blood glucose and insulin profiles were different under the treatment with semilente and NPH insulin. Injection of semilente at bedtime resulted in higher insulin and lower blood glucose values during the second part of the night. The authors concluded that semilente injected at bedtime can prevent the early morning rise in blood glucose in type 1 diabetic patients.

The morning blood glucose levels were significantly lower with semilente compared to NPH insulin, and, as shown in figure 3, night blood glucose profiles were also significantly different.

Hypoglycemia Unawareness

At times insulin users do not recognize that their blood sugar is too low. Not recognizing hypoglycemic symptoms is dangerous and can have serious consequences such as behavioral changes, depression, a lower of quality of

[3] Teuscher A, Mosimann M, de Marco D: Semilente zur Bettzeit reduziert den Schweregrad nächtlicher Hypoglykämien. Oral presentation at the annual meeting of the DDG (Deutsche Diabetes-Gesellschaft), Munich, May 2000.

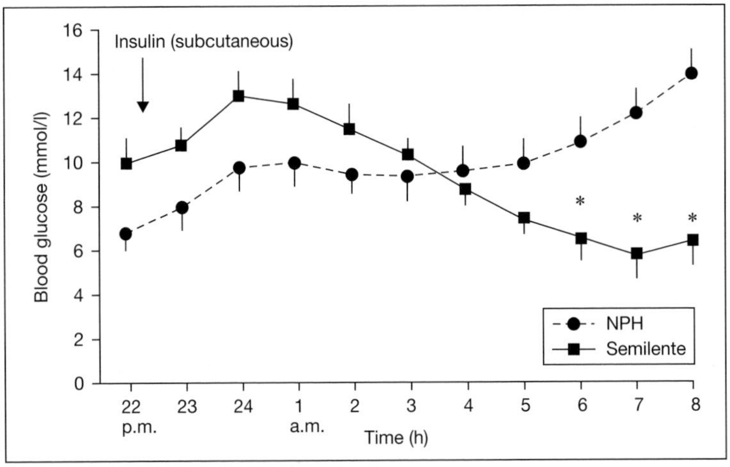

Fig. 3. Overnight blood glucose profile during treatment with NPH insulin or semilente given at bedtime (n = 10) [10]. * = Significant difference.

life, traffic accidents and death. Studies using continuous glucose monitoring suggest the number of people who experience insulin hypoglycemia unawareness may be as high as 63% in type 1 diabetics [11].

Hypoglycemia unawareness may occur in the following situations:

(1) Missed meal, lack of food
(2) Physical exercise, sudden or of long duration
(3) A previous serious hypoglycemic event, in instances where the adrenal gland has run out of adrenaline. Severe hypoglycemia can damage transport signals from the thalamic brain area to the adrenal gland [12]. Repeated episodes of hypoglycemia may blunt the alarm system [13].
(4) The wrong type of insulin taken by mistake, e.g. short- instead of long-acting insulin
(5) Long duration of diabetes [14]
(6) Older people aged 65 years or older
(7) Too much alcohol
(8) 'Brittle' diabetes
(9) Interaction with other drugs, such as salicylates, sulfa antibiotics and some antidepressants [15]. These drugs present risks that should be addressed by all health care givers.
(10) 'Human' insulin and insulin analogues may diminish the warning signals. This phenomenon, discussed in detail in the next chapter, is termed 'human insulin hypoglycemia unawareness' and may occur in a subset of 10–20% or more users [16].

References

1 Berger W, Teuscher A: Hypoglycaemia unawareness in diabetics transferred from beef/porcine insulin to human insulin. Lancet 1987;ii:382–385.

2 Deary IJ, Hepburn DA, MacLeod KM, et al: Partitioning the symptoms of hypoglycaemia using multi-sample confirmatory factor analysis. Diabetologia 1993;36:771–777.

3 Glaser B, Leibowitz G: Hypoglycemia; in Joslin's Diabetes Mellitus, ed 14. Philadelphia, Lippincott Williams & Wilkins, 2005, pp 1150–1151.

4 Clausen Sjöborn N, Lins PE, Adamson U, Theodorsson E: A comparative study on the hormonal responses to insulin-induced hypoglycaemia using semi-synthetic human insulin and pork insulin in patients with type 1 diabetes mellitus. Diabetic Med 1990;7:775–779.

5 Fisher BM, Gray C, Beastall G, Frier BM: Responses to acute insulin-induced hypoglycaemia in diabetic patients. A comparison of short acting human and porcine insulins. Diab Res 1988;8:1–8.

6 Joslin EP: Diabetic Manual for the Doctor and Patient, ed 9. Philadelphia, Lea & Febiger, 1957, p 48.

7 Robbins DC, Normand EF, Colnes JP: Glucose response of diabetic patients to different carbohydrates. N Engl J Med 1984;310:1388–1389.

8 Sussmann KE: Failure of warning in insulin-induced hypoglycemic reactions. Diabetes 1963;12:38.

9 Letters patent of the AGPD (Arbeitsgemeinschaft für Pädiatrische Diabetologie) to Novo Nordisk, January 21, 2006.

10 Strasser D, Nutzi E, Spinas GA, Berger W: Treatment of early-morning hyperglycemia in type 1 diabetics with amorphous zinc insulin (Semilente) at bedtime. Horm Res 1993;39:173–178.

11 Chico A, Vidal-Rios P, Subira M, Novials A: The continuous glucose monitoring system is useful for detecting unrecognized hypoglycemias in patients with type 1 and type 2 diabetes but is not better than frequent capillary glucose measurements for improving metabolic control. Diabetes Care 2003;26:1153–1157.

12 Amiel SA, Tamborlane WB, Simonson DC, Sherwin RS: Defective glucose counterregulation after strict glycemic control of insulin-dependent diabetes mellitus. N Engl J Med 1987;316:1376–1383.

13 Masharani U, Karam JH: Diabetes Mellitus and Hypoglycemia; in Current Medical Diagnosis and Treatment. New York, Lange Medical Books, 2001, p 1188.

14 Amiel S: Joslin's Diabetes Mellitus, ed 14. Philadelphia, Lippincott, 2005, p 675.

15 Physician's Desk Reference (PDR), ed 59. Montvale, Thompson, 2005, p 1855.

16 Teuscher A, Berger W: Hypoglycaemia unawareness in diabetics transferred from beef/porcine insulin to human insulin. Lancet 1987;ii:382–385.

Hazards of 'Human' Insulin Hypoglycemia

Three Alarming Cases

Since the beginning of insulin treatment in 1922 the most serious acute complication has been hypoglycemia. As displayed in figure 8 in the chapter on Aggressive Marketing of 'Human' Insulin and the Withdrawal of Animal Insulin, it now occurs more frequently following the introduction of intensified treatment in 1976. This is, however, in my view directly related to the intensive marketing of 'human' insulin since its approval in 1982. Instead of 1–2 daily injections of animal insulin, 'human' insulin requires 3–4 or even more injections per day because of its shorter and 'sharper' activity. Animal insulins are characterized by 'softer' pharmacokinetics.

Fortunately, deaths due to insulin reactions are rare. Regardless, insulin hypoglycemia is a dangerous state if not diagnosed and treated promptly, and may result in serious brain damage and, at times, even death. In a British Diabetic Association (BDA; now Diabetes UK) study, which analyzed the deaths of 949 patients with type 1 diabetes between 1972 and 1997, hypoglycemia was responsible for 18% of these deaths in men and 6% in women.[4] 'Human' insulin became available in the UK in 1982 and achieved a market share of over 80% by 1998.

I was alerted to the serious problem with 'human' insulin in 1986 by the distressing case of a 20-year-old pharmacy student who had been treated for 6 years with animal insulin and was moderately well adjusted on it. In 1986, the patient was switched to 'human' insulin at his own request. I remember his case as follows:

M.F., Student

On September 9, 1986, his fasting blood sugar before breakfast was 5.8 mmol/l. The patient had had no hypoglycemic episodes for the last few days. He administered his usual insulin dose of fast-acting and long-acting 'human' insulins at 7:15 a.m. The patient had one slice of bread, a smaller amount than usual because of a 5% urine sugar test. After his normal half-hour run in the afternoon he had a bath and was found unconscious in the bathtub at about 6:00 p.m. by his mother. The bath water was splashed on the floor, apparently a

[4] Presented at the British Diabetic Association (BDA) Medical Conference, April 1999.

result of hypoglycemic convulsions. He was brought to the University Hospital of Bern for a glucose drip after a blood sugar reading of 1.7 mmol/l and was able to leave the following day in good condition. He reported that he had not felt any hypoglycemia warning symptoms.

Two weeks later, with a fasting blood sugar before breakfast of 8.5 mmol/l, he injected himself at 7:10 a.m. with 12 units of normal and 18 units of basal insulin, his standard dose at the time, and ate his usual breakfast. The patient's mother prepared his lunch at 11:30 and reminded him to eat soon. Both parents left the house, assuming that their son would continue to work on his graduate thesis. When his father returned at about 5 o'clock, he found him unconscious on the kitchen floor, next to the table where his mother had placed his food. The food was untouched.

The patient was admitted to the University Hospital of Bern with a blood sugar of 1.0 mmol/l at entry, where, in spite of a rapid glucose drip, he remained in a deep coma. A brain scan showed cerebral edema but no damage or bleeding was ascertained. His blood pressure was normal (120/80) and the blood sugar values were stable for 4 days, between 20 and 30 mmol/l, with intravenous glucose and insulin infusions (52 units in 24 h). After 4 days, since there was no improvement, life support was discontinued at the parents' request and the patient was allowed to die.

Since this death was not deemed to be unusual by the head of the medical department, the case was not reported to the authorities and no autopsy was performed. The medical director of the hospital was at that time president of the Swiss Medical Committee responsible for the registration of drugs. Indeed, he was president when 'human' insulins were approved in Switzerland. The insulin manufacturer (Lilly) showed no interest in this case, which I described in *The Lancet* [1] along with 2 other cases which documented serious side effects in patients switched from animal to 'human' insulin.

P.W., Journalist

In another case, P.W., a 37-year-old journalist who had had type 1 diabetes for 18 years, told a meeting of Swiss experts what had happened to him on November 5, 2001 [oral statement, Parliament Building, Bern, March 8, 2002]. Up until then, his diabetic condition had been well controlled with 'human' insulin, although in the last few years he had not been able to recognize every hypoglycemic event as quickly as he would have liked.

On that evening, his blood sugar level seemed under control. Prior to a dinner at a restaurant with his girlfriend, he injected his usual dose of Humalog insulin. After the meal, he drove back to his apartment. Upon arriving, he detected a slightly increased blood sugar of 12 mmol/l, and injected a further dose of 6 units of fast-acting Humalog. At nighttime, he took his usual Semilente MC insulin and went to bed.

He reported that his memory was essentially erased from the moment he fell asleep and early the next morning he had a feeling that he had taken strong drugs the night before, despite the fact that he had not even had one glass of wine. He lay in bed, feeling as if he was having a severe nightmare. He could not think clearly; he did not know where he was or what he was doing. He said he did not even know how to get out of bed.

This was not just simple hypoglycemia, which could be treated with a few cubes of sugar. There were no warning signs such as sweating, shaking and chills. This hypoglycemic event had led directly to a severe loss of brain function and a significant change in consciousness. It was impossible for him to recall the situation. After aimlessly wandering around in his apartment, he was eventually able, despite severely impaired mobility, to instinctively drag himself to the refrigerator and eat whatever he could lay his hands on. Afterwards, he was still far from a normal state of consciousness.

He spent the next 2 days mostly in bed, passing from hypoglycemia to hyperglycemia. Blood sugar measurements were stored in the memory bank of his blood sugar testing device. He could not remember measuring, but must have done so out of habit, since a record was kept on his meter.

The ringing of his mobile phone brought him back to his senses. It was his girlfriend calling. After he mumbled something incoherently to her, she sensed that something was wrong and called emergency services who rushed him to hospital. He was first asked if he had been taking drugs, a question which was repeatedly posed during the first period of his stay in hospital. The doctors were unsure of how to treat him and he was transferred to the University Hospital of Zürich.

He recovered very slowly. His memory was not functioning properly; in the evening he could not remember who had visited him during the day, so he began writing things down. He jumbled words and his speech was at times inarticulate. When he asked the doctors if his state of mind would improve, the reply was 'maybe'.

That he had experienced hypoglycemia was indicated by a bite mark on his tongue, with ensuing ketoacidosis and loss of consciousness. The doctors decided in retrospect that the hypoglycemia was the patient's own fault and sent him to a diabetes counseling service, which recommended an insulin pump. His HbA1c at the time was 6.5%, which proved that his diabetes had been well managed during the preceding months. Oddly enough, he was told he should raise his HbA1c by 1% over the next few months to avoid hypoglycemia.

The idea of raising his blood sugar levels in order to improve his awareness of hypoglycemia did not make sense to him. The absence of hypoglycemia warning signs over the previous few years seemed important to him. He consulted the author, who did not find fault with the patient, but rather with the insulin he was using. P.W. confirmed that his hypoglycemia awareness had been reduced during the last few years after switching from animal to 'human' insulin.

He went back to porcine insulin for a few months and after a short time ascertained that his hypoglycemia awareness had improved significantly. The warning symptoms returned, and his blood sugar control was far more stable. After a month he was able to reduce his HbA1c level to 5.8%. It was unfortunate that animal insulin was not suggested by the diabetologists at the University Hospital of Zürich.

W.B., Journalist

W.B. was very interested in new developments in diabetes treatment. Although his control had been good when using animal insulins, he wanted to switch to 'human' insulin in the mid-1980s. At the beginning, he seemed to do well, but after a while, he started to have sudden hypoglycemia with disturbed consciousness. He decided to return to his previous insulin scheme and felt well controlled on it.

Some time later he was admitted to the University Hospital of Zürich for pancreas and kidney transplantation. When I transferred him, I emphasized his need for animal insulin, and the dangerous experiences he had had with 'human' insulin. The physician in charge noted down the insulin types and doses that I recommended.

Very serious postoperative complications occurred and W.B. had to stay in hospital longer than expected. When I phoned him, he complained about depression and visual disturbances. He said that everything around him was black. I was worried, as he usually was a cheerful person. When I visited him, I found that he had not been given the animal insulin that I had recommended, but 'human' insulin instead. I complained but the hospital endocrinologist said that only 'human' insulin could be used. Tragically, the patient died shortly thereafter as a consequence of severe hypoglycemia.

The three cases above illustrate common problems reported by patients who use 'human' insulin: hypoglycemia unawareness, unexpected and severe hypoglycemia, depression and visual disturbances. In the cases where the patients returned to animal insulin, these problems were significantly alleviated.

Traffic Accidents

Loss of Psychosomatic Control

People are often unaware of the reactions of their bodies when they are concentrating on what they are doing. This phenomenon is accentuated when

Table 7. Accidents (%) in type 1 and type 2 diabetics compared to nondiabetics [4]

	Type 1 diabetes	Type 2 diabetes	No diabetes
Number of subjects	341	332	363
At least 1 accident	19	12	8
Moving vehicle violation	15	8	10
At least 1 hypoglycemic stupor while driving	18	5	no hypoglycemia

the person is driving and becomes hypoglycemic. As noted, seizures, blurred vision, irrational behavior and aggression are symptoms that something is wrong. A person driving in this state endangers him- or herself as well as others. As shown below, hypoglycemia is second only to alcohol as the most frequent cause of car accidents involving diabetic drivers in Switzerland.

When the driving performance of diabetic drivers was tested in driving simulations, performance declined significantly when the driver's blood sugars dropped; with even mild hypoglycemia subjects failed to immediately take corrective action [2]. A 2002 report by the US Federal Motor Carrier Safety Administration (FMCSA) concluded that 'the risk of an accident due to mild hypoglycemia might be suggested to be 1.5 to 3 times higher than that seen under normal driving conditions' [3].

Type 1 diabetics are at higher risk of experiencing hypoglycemia compared to type 2 diabetics, so it is hardly surprising that they are significantly more likely to experience a driving-related mishap (table 7).

Studies on the frequency of accidents caused by diabetics are compromised because of inadequate data. At the time of an accident experienced drivers will be careful not to disclose that they take drugs for diabetes if the police do not ask, since they are concerned about losing their driver's license. Indeed the number of diabetics involved in traffic violations may be considerably underestimated.

Advice to Diabetic Drivers [5–7]

- Keep fast-acting carbohydrate in the vehicle and within easy reach, for example in the pocket of the driver's door.
- Test your blood sugar before driving and at regular intervals (every 2h) during long journeys. Do not drive if your blood glucose is below 4mmol/l. Eat 15–20g of carbohydrate and measure again after 20min if the blood sugar is below 5mmol/l.
- Enter your blood sugar levels in a log or use a testing device with a storage function.

- Take regular meals and breaks on long journeys.
- If a reaction occurs, pull to the roadside and stop immediately, withdraw the engine key, take carbohydrates and wait 30 min before continuing or let a fellow passenger drive.
- Do not drive while your insulin regimen is being changed but wait until the adjustment is complete.
- Consider changing your insulin if your diabetes is not controlled satisfactorily.

Accidents with 'Human' Insulin

G.F., Construction Foreman

During a hospital stay G.F.'s insulin was changed from porcine to 'human' by the hospital's diabetologist. He was given no information about any possible unexpected adverse effects linked to the new insulin treatment. On a clear November day, he got into a colleague's car at the construction site where he worked and drove off to the next village to buy a snack. When he got there, he bought whatever he happened to get his hands on. Without any particular idea in mind, he came out with cold cuts, meat, bread, and different kinds of mineral water, fruit and other food, but he did not eat or drink anything. Normally he would not react so rashly. On the way back, shortly before he reached his destination, symptoms hit him, as he said, 'out of the blue – like lightning'. The car crashed into the right-hand barrier.

When he was admitted to hospital, he was found to have a blood sugar level of 1.5 mmol/l, which explained his loss of control. After receiving a glucose infusion, G.F. was released from hospital the same day. He came to the Bern Diabetes Centre to be transferred back to animal insulin and subsequently regained confidence in his ability to drive safely.

M.W., Teacher

'With "human" insulin I started having concentration problems which especially impaired me in the sports I was doing and were detrimental to my driving. I had to give up playing rugby because I could not cope with the sudden onset of hypoglycemic events during the game. Playing ice hockey presented slightly less of a problem when I was on the rink for short periods of time, since I was able to keep my glucose level relatively constant with sweet drinks. However, I began to notice that my concentration and reaction got worse even when glucose levels measured normal. I started having symptoms of confusion, which displayed themselves in the form of trance-like states and disordered motor coordination. I was no longer able to grasp the meaning of things in context or see connections between things. As a result, I was unable to judge situations for what they were.

This problem became most evident when I was driving in that I was no longer able to make reliable judgements about road conditions that were a bit out of the ordinary, and I was unable to gauge distances, the gradient on uphill stretches and bends in the road. One day when I was driving to work, it was snowing heavily and there were about four inches of snow on the road. About 200 yards from where I live, the road takes a bend. In that first bend I started skidding and ended up inside of the first floor apartment of a farmhouse. I had been unable to judge the road conditions for what they were. Even though I was perfectly aware that there was snow on the road, somehow I failed to make the connection between that and adapting my driving style. It was as if I had been in a trance or completely drunk and I had been driving in snow at the same speed I would normally be driving at if the roads were dry.

For me, using "human" insulin meant being nervous all the time and feeling under constant stress because I could not tell the difference between concentration problems that arose as a result of normal tiredness or overwork and those that were signs of an oncoming hypo. Every time a hypo occurred I would become terrified. That is why I asked my physician to change me back to the animal insulin I was used to and had felt comfortable with. From that day on I lost my disturbing and dangerous behavior and had back my old signs of hypo warning' [pers. commun. by the patient].

F.W., Administrator

'My father and I were driving to B.; my father was at the wheel. It was about 2 hours after a usual lunch at home. We were chatting about the new car, which my father was about to get. Suddenly he changed to the fast lane. He went so far to the left that he was driving close to the crash barrier. As I drew his attention to it he shouted gruffly that I shouldn't tell him how to drive. Suddenly he drove right up to the crash barrier. "Are you mad" I shouted, but just at that moment the car collided with the crash barrier, and skidded back onto the road. For a moment it seemed to stay steady but then it skidded towards the right-hand embankment and the car somersaulted. We got out of our seats and crawled out of the car.

Later we reconstructed the accident for the police and my father insisted that he had noticed no sign of fatigue or limited awareness. I too realized only later that my father caused the accident during hypoglycemia, and I had been unaware of any changes in him.'[5]

F.W. had used 'human' insulin for several years before the accident, and there had been no reason for him to change his treatment before then. The court ruled that he was not guilty of a crime since there was no warning of hypoglycemia unawareness in the package insert and he knew nothing about the possible adverse reactions associated with 'human' insulin. In the mean-

[5] Statement by F.W.'s son.

time, he changed to porcine insulin and kept driving without further problems of this nature.

H.M., Housewife: Driving in Semiconscious State

'I had taken my usual insulin dose, according to the regimen I had been using for more than half a year. I had an appointment with my hairdresser at 2 o'clock. After that, I wanted to drive to the city. I stopped at a red light and now remember nothing until I reached a dead end after about half an hour, where I drove backwards and tipped over a slope. I got out of the car unharmed and went to the closest house. The owner gave me tea with sugar and brought me to the police station. They made a breath test because I acted like a drunk. I then realized that I had been driving more than 20 kilometers through the city and four villages far into the mountains. I did have sugar in the car, but it had not occurred to me to take some.

After contacting a physician, the police let me go home. My car had to be lifted by crane back to the road. After driving home, I collapsed in my garage. I was desperate. Nobody could tell me why I didn't feel the usual signs of hypoglycemia, even at blood sugar levels as low as 1.6 mmol/l. I was sent to the outpatient's department in Bern, where they told me to "be more careful", and that at least I did test my blood sugar before driving, which was good. Then, I found a diabetologist who suggested a transfer back to porcine insulin. The warning signs returned, I was able to avoid severe hypoglycemia and to keep on driving' [pers. commun. by the patient].

Auto Accident Research

Investigations at the Zürich Institute of Legal Medicine show that an increasing number of accidents occur when blood sugars are below 2.8 mmol/l. In 1993, only 4 accidents following insulin hypoglycemia were recorded but in 2000 there were 20, at a time when the overall number of traffic accidents was decreasing. In 1998, hypoglycemia was second only to alcohol as the cause of 'driving in a disturbed or fit-like state of consciousness' in diabetic drivers (fig. 4).

Dr. Rolf Seeger, the physician in charge of returning drivers' licenses to diabetics after their involvement in an accident, recorded an increase in the accidents of diabetic drivers during the period from 1993 to 2004. Although he refused to link this marked increase to 'human' insulin, he admitted that there are drivers who state that they have regained awareness of hypoglycemic symptoms after changing to animal insulin.[6]

In traffic inquiries questions are not systematically asked about diabetes, oral antidiabetic drugs or the kind of insulin used, so that there is little

[6] Oral statements, Postgraduate Diabetes Meeting, spring 2002, Lucerne.

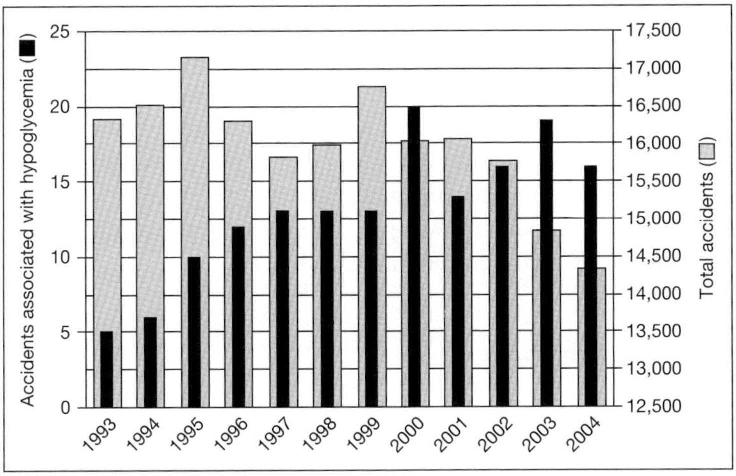

Fig. 4. Traffic accidents in the Canton of Zürich [data from R. Seeger (accidents associated with hypoglycemia) and the Kantonspolizei Zürich (total accidents)].

substantial data to connect accidents with 'human' insulin. However, the fact that the market share in Switzerland of human and analogue insulins in 2000 was already more than 90% suggests that most cases of disturbed consciousness due to insulin were caused by these products.

Legal Aspects of Accidents with Hypoglycemia

In 1994, a diabetic driver in Southern Germany had an unexpected hypoglycemic reaction and caused an accident in which one woman was badly hurt and another one was killed [8]. When the court refused to initiate criminal proceedings against the driver by terming the incident an 'illness-induced blackout', there was an indignant outcry among the people affected. Since the man was using 'human' insulin, the author was asked to discuss in writing the possible relation between his insulin and the accident. The judge did not include my paper in the record, but nevertheless decided in favor of the driver. The medical director of the Bad Mergentheim Diabetes Academy in Germany, the late Professor Bergis, said that the verdict was correct legally but wrong medically.

British law describes accidents caused by insulin treatment as 'self-inflicted', so that the responsibility for hypoglycemia lies with the patient. This is certainly correct in cases where diabetics do not take the usual precautions but one cannot blame a patient for a mistake if he or she has not been told about the dangerous side effects of 'human' insulin. In many cases, such diabetics have a previous history of many severe hypoglycemic events, which ought to alert doctors treating them to problems of low blood sugar. In these circumstances, I believe that a trial of animal insulin should be proposed.

More than 50 car accidents are on file with the author and we have on record only one hypoglycemic accident with a diabetic car driver that occurred before the introduction of 'human' insulin, and one of a pump user on porcine insulin. In addition to legal inquiries, diabetics have to come to terms with their own feelings of guilt. Many give up driving out of a sense of responsibility and thus lose a great part of their mobility and independence.

The 'Dead-in-Bed' Syndrome

The 'dead-in-bed' syndrome occurs almost exclusively in type 1 diabetics under 40. They go to bed in apparently good health and are found the following morning dead near or on an undisturbed bed. The direct cause of death could be dysrhythmia, a variation of the normal regular heartbeat, which could be compounded by nocturnal hypoglycemia [9].

Among 2,792 autopsies performed on diabetic patients at the New England Deaconess Hospital in Boston during the years 1924–1980, 19 cases (0.7%) of death were ascribed to insulin-induced hypoglycemia. Among 33,330 known deaths of patients of the Joslin Diabetes Clinic, from 1922 to 1979, only 85 (0.26%) were reported on death certificates to be caused by hypoglycemia due to insulin [10].

As described below, there appears to have been an increase in the dead-in-bed syndrome since the availability of 'human' insulin.

A Case of 'Dead-in-Bed' Syndrome

J.B., Student

'From October 1990 on, our 24 years old son J.B. lived alone in M. as a student. His type 1 diabetes was diagnosed in 1975 and he was treated with 'human' insulin starting in 1982. From November 1987 to his death in 1994 he had about 20 severe hypoglycemic events, sometimes with convulsions and loss of consciousness, usually at night between 2 and 3:30 a.m. We [his parents] or the emergency doctor often had to inject him with glucagon. He was hospitalized several times' [pers. commun. of J.B.'s parents, 1994].

In 1994, he did not wake up from one of these hypoglycemic attacks. His parents tried to call him several times and finally called the police. The officers found him in a sleeping position with no signs of a break-in or suicide, so there was no postmortem. After his death, J.B.'s parents allowed his electronic diabetes diary to be analyzed. The insulin doses as well as the blood sugar levels had been normal the day of his death.

Two years later, the couple was alerted to the dead-in-bed syndrome in an article published in *Subkutan*, a magazine published by the German Diabetic Federation [11]. They saw parallels between the case of their son and other cases in Switzerland described in the article. They wanted the doctors who had treated him to make it clear whether 'human' insulin could possibly be the cause of his sudden death. The parents took their questions about the cause of their son's death to Professor Peter Hürter of Hanover, but their questions remained unanswered. The parents also recalled that Professor Hürter told them of another young diabetic who died unexpectedly in bed at night.

Their direct questions to the manufacturing company, Novo Nordisk, also failed to provide a satisfactory answer, allegedly because German law controlling drug advertising forbids giving product information to the public. The family doctor's questions were answered by Novo Nordisk as follows: 'Although a working group[7] postulates that pork and "human" insulin have a different ability to pass the blood-brain barrier, there is no indication at present that the cognitive functions of the brain during low blood sugar differ according to the use of various insulin species'.[8]

A letter from the couple to the German *Diabetes Journal* was refused for publication by the Chief Editor and the president of the German Diabetes Association, Professor Eberhard Standl of Munich, on the grounds that it contained many incorrect assumptions and would stir up anxiety. The parents reacted angrily by declaring that: 'Medical problems are swept under the carpet and put young people – a minority of 7% – how comforting! – in an early grave' [12].

The 'Dead-in-Bed' Syndrome at Guy's Hospital

Dr. Patrick Toseland, a physician and pathologist at Guy's Hospital in London, is also a coroner for Greater London and the Southern United Kingdom. In 1989, Dr. Toseland reported that from 1985 to 1989, there was a rise in unexpected deaths among younger type 1 diabetics, as displayed in table 8].

Out of 22 cases in 1989, 9 were under 35 years old and 14 definitely had used 'human' insulin. Three had used 'human' and pork insulin, and it could not be determined which type of insulin they had used before their deaths. In 5 cases, the type of insulin was unknown. In all cases, other causes of death (including insulin overdoses) were ruled out. The patients had simply been found dead in bed. In two cases, when blood sugar could be measured within the critical time of half-an-hour after death, a hypoglycemic value was found.

[7] Thesis of Horst-Lorenz Fehm, neurologist at the University of Lübeck.

[8] Letter from Novo Nordisk to J.B.'s family doctor, 1994.

Table 8. Sudden or unexplained death in younger type 1 diabetics [Toseland, pers. commun., September 17, 1998]

Year	Total deaths investigated by coroner	Sudden or unexplained deaths of type 1 diabetics
1985	856	2
1986	762	4
1987	803	3
1988	774	9
1989	612[a]	22[a]

[a] 10 months only.

Insulin manufacturers explained they had not recorded sudden increases in the number of adverse drug events, but none of the cases Dr. Toseland investigated had been reported to the Committee for Safety of Medicines (now the Commission on Human Medicines).

Since he had seen several reports of altered hypoglycemia warning symptoms on 'human' insulin [13–15] Dr. Toseland made his observations public [16]. The media in the UK relayed the story. Even the BDA was 'very concerned about a number of recent reports of sudden unexpected deaths of apparently healthy young people with insulin-dependent diabetes' [17]. After a 2-min interview on the BBC, Dr. Toseland was widely criticized for having made his observations public. In 1989, an article published in *The Economist* argued that, even though the reasons for the sudden increase in the number of hypoglycemic deaths were not known, 'a case can be made for withdrawing the drug ['human' insulin] from the mass market where alternatives are available' [18]. Comments such as these caused a flurry of activity on Wall Street, and sent the value of Lilly shares into a steep dive. Subsequently, Dr. Toseland went to the US in response to the request by the FDA to discuss his findings.

Further Investigations of the 'Dead-in-Bed' Syndrome

In the UK (excluding Scotland), a 1-year observational study was performed in 1989 to evaluate the significance of the dead-in-bed syndrome in insulin-dependent diabetics. Fifty deaths that seemed sudden or unexpected were investigated. In 22 cases, ketoacidosis (which can be a consequence of a hypoglycemic event with loss of consciousness), suicide, self-poisoning with alcohol and drugs and other defined causes could be excluded as a cause of death. Most of those 22 diabetics had gone to bed in good health, in none were anatomical lesions found, and their diabetes had been uncomplicated and well-controlled in most cases. Treatment with 'human' insulin was common to all [19]. This study supports the diagnosis of sudden death associated with 'human' insulin, as none of these cases was linked to animal insulin.

During the years 1988–1990, researchers Søvik and Thordarson from the University Pediatric Clinic of Bergen, Norway, observed four cases of unexpected deaths in young type 1 diabetic patients. All patients were found dead in an undisturbed bed, after having been in apparently good health the evening before. No cause of death was established, and autopsies were not informative. All 4 patients had been on 'human' insulin and this prompted the investigators to perform an observational study [20] on 'human' insulin hypoglycemia deaths during the period of enforced transfer from highly purified animal to 'human' insulin.

In this study, 240 deaths from all causes in diabetics up to age 40 were found in the period from 1981 to1990. Sixteen of these cases fulfilled the criteria of the dead-in-bed syndrome. Twelve of the patients were reported as having had frequent episodes of hypoglycemia, with nocturnal episodes in 10 cases. There was apparently an increasing incidence of unexplained deaths during the study period, with 12 of 16 cases occurring during the compulsory switch from animal insulin to 'human' insulin, a practice heavily promoted by Novo Nordisk and encouraged by the public health services in Norway.

The conclusion by Søvik and Thordarson 4 years later [21] was that: 'The causes are by definition unknown, but a plausible theory is a death in hypoglycemia, since a history of nocturnal hypoglycemia is noted in most cases.' The rise in the number of deaths in Norway ran parallel to a radical and abrupt switch from the whole range of animal to 'human' insulins throughout Scandinavia. The dead-in-bed syndrome in younger diabetic patients in Norway accounted for about 7% of all deaths among diabetics under the age of 40. At first glance these figures did not seem to be very important to the study's authors, yet the circumstances certainly arouse concern.

The investigations in the UK, Norway and Switzerland on the dead-in-bed syndrome suggested a connection between the use of 'human' insulin and death in younger diabetic patients. In an attempt to disprove such a connection, the Danish diabetologists Borch-Johnsen (who was affiliated with Novo Nordisk) and Helweg-Larsen identified 226 cases of younger insulin-treated diabetics under age 50 who died between 1982 and 1988, a period during which the market share of 'human' insulin increased from 0.2 to 70%. In 98 cases, the cause of death could not be determined, including 51 cases where the patients were found dead in bed. The authors concluded that there was no connection between the introduction of 'human' insulin and increasing mortality in younger insulin-dependent diabetics [22].

The Danish study suffers from an obvious conflict of interest because one of the scientists involved was so closely associated with Novo Nordisk. It is also disturbing that the evidence identified in earlier studies already cited certainly indicated that the dead-in-bed syndrome presented a real danger to patients. A conclusive diagnosis of the dead-in-bed syndrome is difficult because it is next to impossible to obtain accurate blood sugar measurements after death has occurred. This suggests that the syndrome may occur more often than suspected and that more warnings are needed to alert patients, their families and their physicians.

In both the British [19] as well as the Norwegian [21] study it is a question of 'only' 6–7% of all deaths among diabetics under the age of 40. In a study of mortality in diabetic patients during the first 10 years of the disease conducted by Wibell et al. [23] and published in 2001, hypoglycemia or hypoglycemia and ketoacidosis per se played a relatively small role compared with other causes of death, but 31% of the 58 patients who died exhibited these symptoms prior to death. The study identified a single case of unexplained dead-in-bed syndrome.

All patients who are at special risk of severe hypoglycemia should be identified and informed. As the dead-in-bed syndrome is a result of nighttime hypoglycemia, patients who live and sleep alone should be brought into a social network. Furthermore, in my experience previous episodes of 'human' insulin hypoglycemia unawareness are likely to predict the occurrence of the syndrome.

During the first 20 years of my professional experience treating over 20,000 diabetics on animal insulin, there were no unexpected sudden deaths and I believe that the life of many young diabetics using 'human' insulin could have been saved if the problems had been recognized earlier. Among diabetics who do not recognize hypoglycemia when they are affected by it, it is imperative that animal insulin be tried. In many cases the classic warning symptoms such as sweating, tremor and hunger will return if animal insulin is used. I believe that it is the responsibility of physicians and diabetic organizations to inform patients and thereby enable them to make an informed choice about insulins.

Violence and Emotional Instability

Introduction

That low blood sugar can cause bad moods can be seen even in nondiabetic people when they are hungry. In diabetics, this may become what is called 'hypoglycemic automatism', which occurs when patients are no longer aware of what they are doing on a conscious level, leading to accidents and at times violent behavior. The brain is known to be dependent on the equilibrium of hormones in the body. Therefore, the effect of hypoglycemia on the brain and the relationship between diabetes and psychological disorders such as depression are subjects of ongoing research.

Two Cases of Murder with 'Human' Insulin

A.P., Occupation Unknown

A man who stabbed his friend through the heart was allowed to walk free from the court today after the judge cleared him of murder because of his diabetes. Medical reports showed that A.P., aged 37 and diabetic since the age of nine, had too much insulin in his body and suffered a three-hour blackout during which he killed N.T. and attacked police officers.

N.T., 45, died in June this year after being found in a neighboring garden in Stockwell, south London, where he shared a house with A.P. Officers who went to the house in June this year said he 'fought like a man possessed' when they tried to arrest him. When A.P. was interviewed by police he said he had no recollection of the incident.

'There is little doubt that the defendant was suffering from hypoglycemia before, during and after the event', said Mr. Mark Dennis, prosecuting at the Old Bailey. 'He reached a state of hypoglycemic automation.' The condition of hypoglycemia can appear suddenly and instability and mood swings are among the symptoms. J.C., A.P.'s defence attorney, said A.P. was now taking animal insulin instead of 'human' insulin to reduce the chance of him having another attack.

The Recorder of London Justice Michael Hyam recorded a formal not guilty verdict to the murder charge, which the defendant had denied. He said he accepted the medical evidence from Professor Vincent Marks of Surrey University that his behaviour had been out of control. Outside the court, Detective Chief Inspector Richard Taber said: 'The family of the victim has been informed. They are unhappy but understand that circumstances are unique' [24].

A.B., Bricklayer

On the night of July 6, 1991, A.B. stabbed and killed his father-in-law and injured his wife, his mother-in-law and a neighbor. The circumstances that lead to the attack were never fully uncovered. A.B. had been insulin-dependent for 10 years. He had a history of both severe hypoglycemia and drinking beer. It is not known how these episodes affected his brain, or if they were the cause of his mood swings.

His wife had lived in a women's refuge in the 2 months before the attack after he had threatened her with a knife. When he found out that she was visiting her parents, he called several times from a pub, speaking inaccurately. He went home, collected a knife and attacked his wife and her family. After that, he injected himself with a massive dose of insulin, which made it difficult to prove whether or not he was hypoglycemic at the time of the attack. When his blood sugar was measured at the hospital less than an hour after he was arrested it was 1.2 mmol/l. The court discussed whether he lost his conscious control rather due to a hypoglycemic episode than the 'slight to moderate intoxication' by alcohol he had at the same time.

The prosecutor admitted there were rare cases in which insulin-dependent diabetics would get into a state where they were incapable of controlling themselves. He stated this was not such a case, that A.B. had been drunk, armed himself and attacked on purpose.

A.B. finally confessed and was prosecuted for manslaughter, and not for murder. It is difficult to understand why his poor diabetic control had not alarmed physicians before. He routinely administered two daily shots of fast-acting insulin, one in the morning and one at 5 p.m. with doses of about 20 units. Such treatment made him prone to hypoglycemia after midnight. His physician changed his therapy to Actrapid HM in 1987 without justification since A.B. had been well controlled on animal insulin. He was told that his porcine insulin Actrapid MC was no longer available, which was not true. After this change, he lost his hypoglycemia warning signs. Without medical advice, he even gave up driving his motorbike because he had lost these hypoglycemia warning symptoms, indicating that he was concerned about his reactions.

From 1981 to 1987, he was 3 times treated in hospital for severe hypoglycemia . This number increased 5-fold after he switched to 'human' insulin. His wife testified in court that he had been admitted to hospital through the emergency ward at least 40 times from the time he switched insulins until his arrest. In prison, an inmate who had stopped using 'human' insulin suggested that A.B. ask to be transferred to porcine insulin. After requesting to do so several times and being ignored, A.B. changed back to porcine insulin in 1992. Since then he has been well controlled, and his warning signs such as hunger, sweating and restlessness have returned [pers. commun.].

Published Research Studies on Emotional Instability

Studies conducted during the last 20 years have focused on the connection between diabetes and depression and its complications. There is evidence that the increased risk for depressive symptoms detected by these studies could be a result of changes in brain function due to the metabolic changes as a result of diabetes [25]. However, because these studies were done in most facilities after 'human' insulin replaced animal insulin, it is impossible to know whether 'human' insulin has different effects on emotions than animal insulin. Even so I include these studies here because I believe that appropriate studies would indeed indicate that there is a difference.

Having a chronic disease such as diabetes may also influence the tendency to mood disorders. A review by the Karolinska Institute in Sweden of Scandinavian articles on health-related quality of life issues demonstrated that diabetes affects the quality of life through microvascular complications and associated nonvascular comorbidity, and thus adds to the total burden of disease [26].

The impact of hypoglycemia on the brain is a major factor influencing the clinical management of type 1 diabetes mainly in children. Intensive insulin treatment is the most effective strategy for preventing long-term microvascular and neurological complications. Intensive treatment is especially recommended for children, since they do have their whole life ahead of them. Nevertheless intensive insulin therapy is associated with an increased risk of severe hypoglycemia [27].

The study by Rankins et al. [28] was the first to show that acute hypoglycemia has transient effects on neurometabolite and neuropsychological profiles in diabetic children. Unlike the frontal lobe, temporal lobe and basal ganglia changes were minimal, suggesting that neuronal integrity in anterior brain regions is particularly susceptible to acute hypoglycemia. The study suggests that temporal lobes are affected by hypoglycemia, with a recovery of memory skills 6 months later. The increased levels of an amino acid recorded immediately following the seizures may reflect neurodegeneration. Similar findings [29, 30] for event-related potentials and regional cerebral blood flow indicate that frontal regions are activated during acute hypoglycemia. Frontal brain regions are thought to be involved in higher-order cognitive processing, including attention.

As noted by McIntyre et al. [31]:

Bipolar disorder [BD] is a highly prevalent and disabling condition with significant mortality risk from suicide and other unnatural causes. Diabetes mellitus [DM] is also a prevalent multifactorial disease, which imparts substantial illness burden. Preliminary investigations indicate that patients who suffer from bipolar disorder with co-morbid DM have a more severe course and outcome, lower quality of life, higher prevalence of medical co-morbidity and higher cost of illness. Subpopulations of BD patients should be considered at high risk for DM. The prevalence of DM in BD may be three times greater than in the general population. Bipolar disorder populations may be an at-risk group for glucose metabolic abnormalities. Opportunistic screening and vigilance for clinical presentations suggestive of DM is encouraged.

The purpose of this study carried out in Korea was to examine the depressive symptoms of type 2 diabetic patients who were treated with insulin compared to those diabetics treated with oral antidiabetic drugs. A total of 204 outpatients with type 2 diabetes were invited to complete a questionnaire using the Beck depression inventory to measure depressive symptoms. They were divided into an oral drug group and an insulin group, the insulin group including those who used both oral drugs and insulin. Compared to the oral drug group, the insulin group showed a significantly higher frequency of depressive symptoms (48.0 : 27.3%) and of depression (odds ratio 4.38, 95% CI 1.66–11.6, $p = 0.003$). The data thus demonstrated that insulin treatment is related to the presence of depressive symptoms, and more careful psychological support of insulin-treated type 2 diabetic patients is strongly suggested [32].

The manufacturers of antidepressants and the companies which make 'human' insulin may be misdiagnosing diabetic patients with depression rather than with an adverse side effect to the insulin itself. The statistics on depression are notoriously unreliable at the best of times, and in regard to insulin-dependent diabetics this is even more the case. Reports indicate that 'human' insulin is linked to more aggressive behavior, frequent mood swings and loss of memory, conditions which may be alleviated with a switch to animal-sourced insulins. The use of antidepressants to treat patients experiencing these symptoms may be inappropriate.

References

1 Teuscher A, Berger W: Hypoglycaemia unawareness in diabetics transferred from beef/porcine insulin to human insulin. Lancet 1987;ii:382–385.

2 Cox DJ, Gonder-Frederick LA, Kovatchev BP, Julian DM, Clarke WL: Progressive hypoglycemia's impact on driving simulation performance. Occurrence, awareness and correction. Diabetes Care 2000;23:163–170.

3 FMCSA Medical Reports: Cardiovascular Advisory Panel Guidelines for the Medical Examination of Commercial Motor Vehicle Drivers, FMCSA-MCP-02-002, October 2002, part IV, pp 70–92. http://www.fmcsa.dot.gov/Pdfs/insulin4.pdf.

4 Cox DJ, Penberthy JK, Zrebiec J, et al: Diabetes and Driving Mishaps. Frequency and correlations from a multinational survey. Diabetes Care 2003;26:2329–2334.

5 Schweizerische Diabetesgesellschaft: Diabetes & Autofahren: Gute Werte? – Gute Fahrt! 2005.

6 IDDT Newsletter, January 2005, p 9.

7 Deutscher Diabetiker Bund Landesverband Hamburg e.V. Führerschein und Autofahren. http://www.diabetikerbund-hamburg.de/informationen/autofahr.htm 4.2.2005.

8 Haertel F: Tödlicher Blackout. Focus 1994, vol 46, p 44.

9 Weston PJ, Gill GV: Is undetected autonomic dysfunction responsible for sudden death in type 1 diabetes mellitus? The 'dead in bed' syndrome revisited. Diabet Med 1999;16:626–631.

10 Joslin EP: Joslin's Diabetes Mellitus, ed 12. Philadelphia, Lea & Febiger, 1985, p 402.

11 Teuscher, A: Tot-im-Bett-Syndrom. Subkutan July 1996;15:16–17.

12 B.J., B.E.: Letter to the Editor. Subkutan October 1996;15:30.

13 Teuscher A, Berger WG: Hypoglycaemia unawareness in diabetics transferred from beef/porcine insulin to human insulin. Lancet 1987;ii:382–385.

14 Tattersall RB. Drug Ther Bull 1989.

15 Redmond S: Changing to human insulin. Balance 1988;106:66–68.

16 Toseland PA: Editorial. Med Sci Law 1990;30:2.

17 Tattersall R: Diabetes deaths and human insulins. The Guardian, Aug 10, 1989.

18 The human factor: artificial insulin is now available as an alternative to insulin from animals. The Economist, Oct 21, 1989.

19 Tattersall RB, Gill GV: Unexplained deaths of type 1 diabetic patients. Diabet Med 1991;8:49–58.
20 Thordarson H, Søvik O: Dead-in-bed syndrome in young diabetic patients. Diabet Med 1995;12:782–787.
21 Sovik O, Thordarson H: Dead-in-bed syndrome in young diabetic patients. Diabetes Care 1999;22(suppl 2):B40–42.
22 Borch-Johnsen K, Helweg-Larsen K: Sudden death and human insulin: is there a link? Diabet Med 1993;10:255–259.
23 Wibell L, Nyström L, Östman J, Anrqvist H, Blohmé G, Lithner F, Littorin B, Sundkvist G: Increased mortality in diabetes during the first 10 years of the disease. A population-based study (DISS) in Swedish adults 15–34 years old at diagnosis. J Intern Med 2001;249:263.
24 BBC News, Dec 16, 1999.
25 Jacobson AM, et al: Diabetes, the brain, and behavior: is there a biological mechanism underlying the association between diabetes and depression? Int Rev Neurobiol 2002;51:455–479.
26 Wandell PE: Quality of life of patients with diabetes mellitus. An overview of research in primary health care in the Nordic countries. Scand J Prim Health Care 2005;23:68–74.
27 The DCCT Research Group: The effect of intensive treatment of diabetes on the development and progression of long-term complications in insulin-dependent diabetes mellitus. N Engl J Med 1993;329:982.
28 Rankins D, Wellard RM, Cameron F, et al: The impact of acute hypoglycemia on neuropsychological and neurometabolite profiles in children with type 1 diabetes. Diabetes Care 2005;28:2771–2773.
29 Smid HGOM, Trümper BG, Pottaq G, et al: Differentiation of hypoglycaemia induced cognitive impairments: an electrophysiological approach. Brain 1997;120:1041–1056.
30 MacLeod KM, Hepburn DA, Deary IJ, et al: Regional cerebral blood flow in IDDM patients: effects of diabetes and of recurrent severe hypoglycaemia. Diabetologia 1994;37:257–263.
31 McIntyre RS, Konarski JZ, Misener VL, et al: Bipolar disorder and diabetes mellitus: epidemiology, etiology, and treatment implications. Ann Clin Psychiatry 2005;17:83–93.
32 Noh JH, Park JK, Lee HJ, et al: Depressive symptoms of type 2 diabetics treated with insulin compared to diabetics taking oral anti-diabetic drugs: a Korean study. Diabetes Res Clin Pract 2005;69:243–248.

Research Demonstrating that 'Human' and Animal Insulins Are Not the Same

Introduction

It is my opinion that the enthusiasm about the alleged advantages of 'human' insulin leaves many of my colleagues blind to its disadvantages. They have been blinded not only by the drug sponsors' aggressive marketing campaigns but also by work such as the Cochrane review of 2005. This review was based on a meta-analysis of 45 randomized controlled trials, most of which were of 'poor methodological quality', according to the published review [1]. Nonetheless, and against this important caveat, Cochrane reviewers concluded that differences in the effects of animal and 'human' insulin were of no clinical significance.

The purpose of this chapter is to review the clinical and basic scientific research which demonstrates that 'human' and animal insulins have different clinical effects in some type 1 diabetics. Furthermore, studies indicate that there are molecular differences between so-called 'human' insulin and the insulin produced by normal beta cells.

Clinical Research Studies

Problems with hypoglycemia in patients using Humulin insulin were found even before the drug was registered in 1982. The Medical Officer in charge of the FDA's review of Eli Lilly's New Drug Application (NDA) for Humulin [2] was Dr. Henry Miller. In his summary of two studies, Miller notes that hypoglycemia was reported in 61% of type 1 patients and in 81% of type 2 patients during the 2nd month of therapy, declining to 38 and 62%, respectively, after 6 months. He concluded that:

In the insulin-transfer protocol (# 6), the physicians' assessment of general diabetic control indicated slight deterioration of control after transfer from ISP [beef-pork insulin] or PPI [pork insulin] to BHI [biosynthetic human insulin]. Control improved gradually over several months, suggesting that this deterioration is a temporary phenomenon.

In addition to these findings, 7 patients terminated their participation in the two studies (one of them pivotal) for unidentified reasons.

Another clinical trial of 'human' insulin, sponsored by Novo and published in 1982 before the product was approved for general use, was carried out by Clark et al. [3]. It was a double-blind crossover study of 94 diabetics, all established animal insulin users, who were switched to 'human' insulin for 6-week periods. Six patients withdrew during the trial, 3 because of hypoglycemia with 'human' insulin and 3 for reasons unrelated to insulin treatment. While the total number of hypoglycemic episodes was not significantly different between the insulin species, the fact that 3 patients who switched to 'human' insulin were troubled enough by the hypoglycemic episodes to request switching back suggests the symptoms were sufficiently different and worrisome to cause them to withdraw from the study.

A similar early study, undertaken for the registration process in European countries, was conducted in 1982 by Møller-Jensen and Kühl [4]. These investigators compared two 'human' insulins, Actrapid HM and Protaphane HM, to their porcine insulin counterparts in 25 patients. Two dropouts were recorded: one because the patient failed to order new supplies from the hospital and one due to frequent hypoglycemic reactions with 'human' insulin. Since the 'problem continued with the original insulin,... the ractions [sic] were likely the result of insulin overdosage'.

These findings from very early studies may seem minor on the surface. However, they provide an 'early warning' of problems with the new product. Indeed, John Galloway, a clinical investigator for Eli Lilly, reported in 1983 that 3 patients treated in the Lilly clinical research facility felt changes in the nature of hypoglycemic reactions with the 'human' insulin that was being studied. These changes included less perspiration and nervousness, and fewer palpitations than experienced during hypoglycemia on animal insulin. Furthermore, these patients reported unusual symptoms, such as 'fuzzy headedness' and 'weakness in the arms and legs'. In a discussion on differences between counterregulation on 'human' and animal insulin in 1987, J.H. Anderson concluded that since these problems arose only in a subset of patients, the prospective studies then underway might not have detected them [Anderson, pers. commun. at the International Diabetes Federation meeting in Sidney, August 17, 1987].

Another early suggestion that there might be problems with 'human' insulin was provided in 1984 by Professor E.F. Pfeiffer, Director of the Diabetes Department at the University Hospital in Ulm (Germany), who declared:

'I have known diabetic patients who tell me that they are absolutely unaware of it ["human" insulin hypoglycemia], patients who would come into the room and before they could get food, were already unconscious. This is something different because the patients have not encountered this kind of hypoglycemia attack previously. It is something new, and we have to find out why' [5].

As noted in the chapter on Hazards of 'Human' Insulin Hypoglycemia, the unexpected death in 1986 of one of my patients prompted me to look more closely at this problem. The patient, an intelligent pharmacology student who controlled his diabetes with care, chose to switch to the highly touted 'human' insulin with my concurrence. This switch tragically resulted in his death from what I have chosen to term "human" insulin hypoglycemia unawareness'.

My colleagues Willi Berger and Beat Althaus found in 1987 that after changing from 'human' to animal insulin, two thirds of the 39 patients who answered a retrospective questionnaire stated that their ability to recognize hypoglycemia was delayed and less pronounced on 'human' insulin, while one third noticed no difference. Therapy with animal insulin had to be reinstated in 8 patients due to an absence of the warning signals of hypoglycemia [6].

Further scientific research on this topic, performed by Berger and myself [7], was published in *The Lancet*. We studied 176 patients at the universities of Bern and Basel who had switched from animal insulin to 'human' insulin. Of these, 66 reported changes in their symptoms of hypoglycemia, either spontaneously or when responding to a structured questionnaire. The changes were from the 'classic' warning symptoms such as sweating, tremor and hunger (i.e. sympathoadrenal symptoms) to lack of concentration, restlessness, confusion and behavioral changes (i.e. neuroglycopenic symptoms). Seven patients with severe hypoglycemia unawareness on 'human' insulin were switched back to animal insulin, 3 at their own request, and all 7 regained their usual awareness of hypoglycemia.

When we decided to present the results of this study in a national television broadcast in Switzerland, we were massively criticized by the Swiss Diabetes Association:

'... It is irresponsible of the doctors to expose their questionable results publicly and thus make the diabetics feel insecure... no blame whatsoever can for the time being be put on human insulins with regard to the reduced awareness of hypos...' [8].

However, the positive feedback from diabetic patients motivated Matthias Egger and me to publish a follow-up study in *The Lancet* [9] in 1989. We found that 2 years after switching, 34 of the 59 patients under study had switched back to animal insulin several months earlier. The 25 who remained on 'human' insulin continued to experience neuroglycopenic symptoms, but reported that these symptoms were weaker, occurred later and were detected at lower blood glucose levels.

In another publication in *The Lancet* in 1989, Berger et al. [10] confirmed these results in a randomized, double-blind crossover trial. They found classic sympathoadrenal symptoms of hypoglycemia to be significantly more frequent during treatment with animal insulin than with 'human' insulin (41 vs. 20%). In these cases hypoglycemia developed later with 'human' insulin and at lower blood glucose levels, but blood sugars dropped much faster. Thus, the early warning signs of hypoglycemia were delayed, impairing the patient's early recognition and timely treatment. At the end of the trial, 18 of the 32 subjects reported diminished awareness of hypoglycemia during 'human' insulin therapy compared with 6 treated with porcine insulin.

In 1991 Egger et al. [11] reported the results of a randomized controlled double-blind crossover trial performed at the University of Bern in the *British Medical Journal*. In this study, 44 patients reported their hypoglycemic symptoms in a questionnaire. Insulin doses, HbA1c levels and fructosamine concentration were similar during the two treatment periods included in the study. The investigators found that 'human' insulin patients were more likely to report lack of concentration (52 vs. 35%, $p = 0.0003$), restlessness (53 vs. 45%, $p = 0.004$) and were less likely to report hunger (33 vs. 42%, $p = 0.016$) than during treatment with porcine insulin. During 17 episodes involving 13 patients using 'human' insulin and during 6 episodes involving 5 patients on porcine insulin no glucose measurement was performed because of abrupt onset of hypoglycemia.[9] The differences in the pattern of symptoms were similar to those in a second treatment group composed of 12 patients with a history of recurrent hypoglycemic coma and 32 patients without such a history.

The fact that 'human' insulin-induced hypoglycemia elicits a weaker response of adrenaline and other counterregulatory hormones [12, 13] might affect the way diabetics experience hypoglycemia.[10] But pharmacokinetic differences may also explain the variations [Anderson, pers. commun. at the International Diabetes Federation meeting in Sidney, August 17, 1987] since, as noted in the 1993 *British National Formulary*[11], 'human sequence preparations tend to have a more rapid onset and a shorter overall duration' [14]. These differences are also demonstrated in figure 5.

In a matched case-control study by Egger et al. [16] published in the *British Medical Journal* in 1991, hospital admissions for hypoglycemia for the years 1984–1987 were analyzed. During the period under review, the use of 'human' insulin in the region from which subjects were drawn rose from 4 to 59%. The objective was to determine if switching from animal insulin to 'human' insulin was associated with an increased risk of severe hypoglycemia. Case and control admissions were obtained from 8 public hospitals in and around Bern, Switzerland, and 112 cases of hypoglycemia with unconsciousness were found to have been admitted during

[9] Letter of M. Egger to Dr. P.C. Waller, Committee on Safety of Medicine UK, February 23, 1992.

[10] Schweiz. Serum- & Impfinstitut Bern (distributor for Eli Lilly products in Switzerland) in a letter to Swiss diabetologists, July 1984.

[11] The BNF is a publication compiled to provide guidance to health care professionals on prescribing, dispensing and administering medicines.

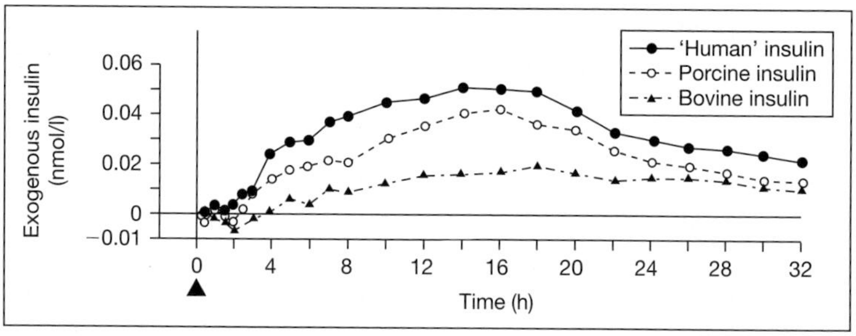

Fig. 5. Pharmacokinetics of different insulin species. Adjusted insulin levels following 'human', porcine and bovine ultralente insulin administration in 6 normal volunteers [15]. Reproduced with permission from John Wiley & Sons, Ltd.

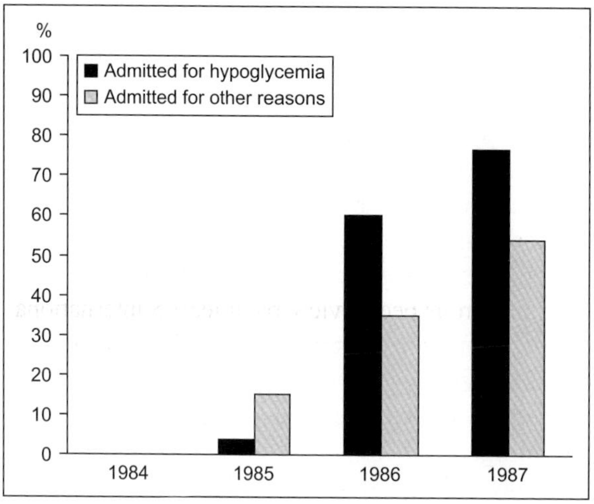

Fig. 6. Analysis by year of rate of admission for hypoglycemia (cases) or other reasons (controls). Use of 'human' insulin is shown on y-axis [16].

that period. The controls were 225 diabetic patients admitted to the same hospitals for reasons other than hypoglycemia. We found that treatment with 'human' insulin at admission was more common in cases than controls ($p = 0.003$) (fig. 6).

Other risk factors for severe hypoglycemia were a history of hypoglycemic coma (rate ratio of history to no history 3.8, 2.3–6.4) and good glycemic control (rate ratio of good to poor control 3.9, 1.4–7.5). With multivariate analysis, the increase in rate ratio associated with use of 'human' insulin rose to 3.0 (1.4–6.4).

In a similar study conducted at the University of Southampton in England and reported in 1992 [17], more patients who were admitted to hospital with hypoglycemia (66.1%) had been taking 'human' insulin compared with the matched control group (44.7%). Diabetics who took 'human' insulin were 3.12 times more likely to have suffered from severe hypoglycemia compared with those on animal insulin.

These and other studies suggest that switching from natural to 'human' insulin in the 1980s was associated with an increased risk of severe hypoglycemia among diabetic patients (compare fig. 8 in the chapter on Aggressive Marketing of 'Human' Insulin and the Withdrawal of Animal Insulin). Indeed, this finding was reflected in the 'boxed warning' included on the label of Humulin insulin by the manufacturer, Eli Lilly, and approved by the FDA (see the chapter on Aggressive Marketing of 'Human' Insulin and the Withdrawal of Animal Insulin).

The FDA's approval of Humulin insulin was described by the reviewers as 'an epochal event [which] will permit for the first time anywhere in the world the marketing of a drug produced by recombinant DNA technology' [2]. Therefore, it was not surprising that the serious problems found in randomized, controlled studies of the new drug stimulated heated discussions within the medical community. Manufacturers also became very much involved since the successful marketing of 'human' insulin was of great importance not only financially, but also for the future of biopharmaceuticals generally. Some medical advisors, possibly influenced by such concerns, criticized medical journals for publishing these studies, implying that they did not meet proper standards. In response, Richard Smith, chief editor of the *British Medical Journal*, declared that all of the studies published in his prestigious magazine had undergone a rigorous peer review by at least 8 international experts and were 'as scientifically sound as anything else published on this subject, and considerably more sound than most of what has been published' [18].

Novo Nordisk entered this controversy directly by supporting an Australian study by Colagiuiri et al. [19] that was published in *The Lancet* in 1992. The second author, J.J. Miller, an employee of Novo Nordisk, undoubtedly played a major role in the design of the study and the analysis of the findings. But authors were not required to report such conflicts of interest at that time.

At first glance the study appears to be a standard double-blind crossover study, done to investigate differences between animal and 'human' insulin in the frequency and characteristics of hypoglycemic episodes. Fifty patients were referred to the authors by their physicians because of complaints about a lack of awareness of hypoglycemia with 'human' insulin. They had had diabetes for a mean of 20 years and 70% had good or acceptable glycemic control. HbA1c values were obtained but not validated in a central laboratory and therefore not published. Each patient was treated in a double-blind manner for four 1-month periods, 2 with 'human' and 2 with animal insulin, in random order.

The authors concluded that they found no statistically significant differences between the insulin species with respect to glycemic control or the frequency, timing, severity, or awareness of hypoglycemia. They reported that the mean percentage of hypoglycemic episodes associated with reduced or absent awareness was 64% for 'human' insulin and 69% for animal insulin.

In my view, and in the view of colleagues who submitted their comments as letters to the editor of *The Lancet*, one cannot conclude from this study that all diabetics who use 'human' insulin in real-life situations do so safely. Egger and Smith [20] found fault with the randomization of subjects, the lack of quality control in the laboratories used, and the fact that hypoglycemia was recognized at lower glucose concentrations with 'human' than with animal insulin.

As I stated in a letter to the editor of *The Lancet,* 'Colagiuri's study is of little help [21]. It is not the frequency of mild hypoglycemia that is of primary concern'. Similarly, Ernst von Kriegstein wrote, 'As practicing clinicians, we nevertheless value the experience of our patients more than Colagiuri's data' [22].

The 'real world' in which diabetics live differs significantly from a drug company's clinical environment, and it was this world that was overlooked in the Colagiuri study.

Another double-blind randomized crossover study from London published in the *British Medical Journal* the following year [23] was to some extent similar to the Novo Nordisk study but was even less comparable to real-life situations because some of the work was done in the controlled setting of a clinical investigation unit of a teaching hospital and involved 'clamping', as described below.

The subjects were 17 patients with insulin-dependent diabetes mellitus of more than 5 years' duration who had reported altered hypoglycemia awareness episodes within the preceding 3 months and subsequent to switching to 'human' insulin. Two patients that were seen by the recruiting center refused to participate in the study because they did not want to take 'human' insulin again. The research team compared the subjects' awareness of hypoglycemia when using 'human' and animal insulin. In addition they measured the subjects' physiological responses to 'clamping' during a 5-hour controlled fall in blood sugar at a certain level. Clamping is a laboratory procedure used to determine how much glucose is required to keep the blood sugar level constant when insulin is given.

The investigators concluded that under these conditions, glycemic control did not differ between the two species of insulin, with 136 hypoglycemic episodes (8 severe) linked to 'human' insulin and 149 episodes (9 severe) to animal insulin (95% confidence interval –4 to 2.5, $p = 0.63$). During controlled hypoglycemia with the clamp the mean adrenaline response was 138 nmol/l/240 min for both insulins; neurohormonal responses were triggered at 3.0 mmol/l (SE 0.2) versus 3.1 mmol/l (SE 0.2) of glucose for adrenaline and 2.5 mmol/l (SE 0.1) versus 2.5 mmol/l (SE 0.1) for subjective awareness.

My criticism of this study is the same as my criticism of the Novo Nordisk study. However, I would add that a slow fall in blood sugars over 5 h is certainly not comparable to the experiences of type 1 diabetic patients in real-life

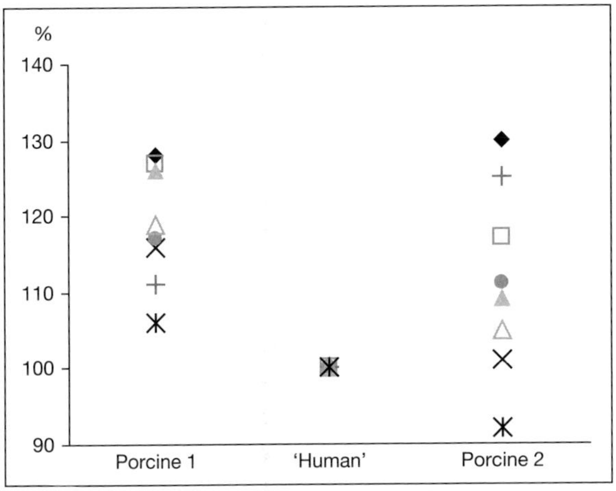

Fig. 7. EEG power density during sleep with porcine/'human'/porcine insulin in 8 diabetic subjects shown by the 8 symbols. Note that the readings on 'human' insulin are identical [24].

conditions when the life-threatening problems described by the majority of investigators can occur within minutes or even seconds.

Basic Research Studies

Clinical laboratory research and studies in molecular biology have also demonstrated differences between 'human' and animal insulin. In a study published in 1998 in *Sleep* we found a significant drop in brain signal activity in the thalamic area in patients on 'human' insulin [24]. The study was performed with near-normoglycemic control in 8 type 1 diabetic patients, all established porcine insulin users with a history of unconsciousness relating to 'human' insulin hypoglycemia. Sleep EEGs were done in 3 consecutive sessions of 2 nights each. During the first 2 nights the subjects were given porcine insulin, during the second 2 nights 'human' insulin, and during the third 2 nights, porcine insulin again. We found that porcine and 'human' insulins have different effects on the power densities of the EEGs during sleep, as shown in figure 7.

We concluded that some brain functions are affected differently by the two types of insulin. There is evidence that such differences in the neurophysiological function are also seen when blood glucose levels drop to hypoglycemic levels. In a study published in 1990, Kern et al. [25] found that auditory and visual responses were significantly weaker during the first 20 min of hypoglycemia inducted by 'human' insulin as distinct from the reaction after porcine insulin. The investigators concluded that: '...human and pork insulin-induced hypoglycemia differ in their actions'.

Pharmacological studies by Galloway et al. [26], all employees of Eli Lilly, clearly demonstrate that 'human' insulin is absorbed faster than animal insulin, thus increasing the serum insulin concentration after subcutaneous injections. Studies also show that animal insulin is more lipophilic than 'human' insulin which is more hydrophilic [27, 28] resulting in a faster cerebral accumulation of animal insulin [29].

Inquiries into the molecular structure of 'human' and animal insulins have also demonstrated differences. Even though the amino acid structure of 'human' insulin may appear to be an exact copy of the insulin produced by nondiabetics, it is not the product of a natural system and therefore has different attributes. Richard Lewontin [30], Professor of Biochemistry at Harvard University, observed: 'genes do not make proteins, they only specify the sequence of amino acids in the protein'.

Lewontin and Fuller [30] also noted that when 'human' insulin was first produced by bacteria:

...it turned out that the bacteria folded the molecule incorrectly, producing an insulin that was physiologically inactive and therefore useless as a drug. To solve this problem, the manufacturers harvest the incorrectly folded protein from the bacteria, treat it with heat to unfold it, and then refold it by an industrial process that is a trade secret.

Over the last 30 years studies have been unable to identify any clear advantages of the use of 'human' insulin over animal insulin in the treatment of diabetes. A number, in fact, have pointed to problems associated with diminished hypoglycemia warning signals, a potentially life-threatening situation. Anecdotal evidence in the form of adverse effects reported by patients has simply been ignored or dismissed by many practitioners, regulators and manufacturers. As we will see in the next chapter, clearly evidence that called for caution was unable to halt or influence the marketing of 'human' insulin worldwide.

References

1 Richter B, Neises G: 'Human' insulin versus animal insulin in people with diabetes mellitus. Cochrane Database Syst Rev 2005;1:CD003816. DOI: 10.1002/14651858.CD003816.pub2.

2 US Food and Drug Administration: NDA 18,780 and 18,781, Medical Officers' Review (MOR) of New Drug Application (NDA), July 20, 1982.

3 Clark AJ, Adeniyi-Jones RO, Knight G, Leiper JM, Wiles PG, Jones RH, Keen H, MacCuish AC, Ward JD, Watkins PJ, Cauldwell JM, Glynne A, Scotton JB: Biosynthetic human insulin in the treatment of diabetes. A double-blind crossover trial in established diabetic patients. Lancet 1982;ii:354–357.

4 Møller-Jensen B, Kühl C: Investigation of the safety and efficacy of Actrapid HM and Protaphane HM. Data on file Hvidore Hospital, Klampenborg, 1982/1983.

5 L'Etang H-JC: Diabetes Mellitus. Achievements and Scepticism. Int Congr Symp Ser No 77. London, Royal Society of Medicine, 1984, p 141.
6 Berger WG, Althaus BU: Reduced awareness of hypoglycemia after changing from porcine to human insulin in IDDM. Diabetes Care 1987;10:260.
7 Teuscher A, Berger WG: Hypoglycaemia unawareness in diabetics transferred from beef/porcine insulin to human insulin. Lancet 1987;ii:382–385.
8 Kappeler D (President of the Medical Committee of the Swiss Diabetes Association): Television transmission SF DRS, September 24, 1987. (Translation taken from Dejgaard A: Awareness of hypoglycaemia during treatment with human insulin, confidential report, Novo, October 16, 1987.)
9 Teuscher A, Egger M: Human insulin hypoglycaemia unawareness. Lancet 1989;1:1072.
10 Berger W, Keller U, Honegger B, Jaeggi E: Warning symptoms of hypoglycaemia during treatment with human and porcine insulin in diabetes mellitus. Lancet 1989;i:1041–1044.
11 Egger M, Smith GD, Teuscher AU, Teuscher A: Influence of 'human' insulin on symptoms and awareness of hypoglycemia: a randomized double blind crossover trial. BMJ 1991;303:622–626.
12 Rosak C, Althoff PH, Enzmann F, Schoffling K: Comparative studies on intermediary metabolism and hormonal counterregulation following human insulin (recombinant DNA) and purified pork insulin in man. Diabetes Care 1982;5(suppl 2):82–89.
13 Schluter KJ, Enzmann F, Kerp L: Different potencies of biosynthetic human and purified porcine insulin. Horm Metab Res 1983;15:271–274.
14 BNF (British National Formulary), No 25. British Medical Association and the Royal Pharmaceutical Society of Great Britain, London, March 1993, p 255.
15 Owens DR, Vora JP, Heding LG, Luzio S, Ryder RE, Atiea J, Hayes TM: Human, porcine and bovine ultralente insulin: subcutaneous administration in normal man. Diabet Med 1986;3:326–329.
16 Egger M, Smith GD, Imhoof H, Teuscher A: Risk of severe hypoglycaemia in insulin treated diabetic patients transferred to human insulin: a case control study. BMJ 1991;303:617–621.
17 Iles S: Thesis/Project University of Southampton, General Hospital Wessex, Medical Library book No. 93131296, 1992.
18 Smith R: Letter. Novo Nordisk Bull, Jan 1992, p 21.
19 Colagiuri S, Miller JJ, Petocz P: Double-blind crossover comparison of 'human' and porcine insulins in patients reporting lack of hypoglycemia awareness. Lancet 1992;339:1432–1435.
20 Egger M, Smith GD: Letter to the editor. Lancet 1992;340:301.
21 Teuscher A: Letter to the editor. Lancet 1992;340:301–302.
22 von Kriegstein E: Letter to the editor. Lancet 1992;340:302.
23 Maran A, Lomas J, Archibald H, et al: Double-blind clinical and laboratory study of hypoglycemia with 'human' and porcine insulin in diabetic patients reporting hypoglycemia unawareness after transferring to 'human' insulin. BMJ 1993;306:167–171.
24 Roth C, Landolt HP, Achermann P, Teuscher A, Borbély AA: Human versus porcine insulin in patients with insulin-dependent diabetes mellitus: differences in sleep and the sleep EEG during near-normoglycemia. Sleep 1998;21:92–100.
25 Kern W, Born J, Kerner W, Fehm HL: Different effects of human and porcine insulin-hypoglycaemia induced abnormalities of brainstem sensory function. Clin Phys Biochem 1990;8:122–127.
26 Galloway JA, Root MA, Bergstrom R, Spradlin CT, Howey DC, Fineberg SE, Jackson RL: Clinical pharmacologic studies with human insulin (recombinant DNA). Diabetes Care 1982;5(suppl 2):13–22.
27 Markussen, J, Damguard U, Johansen NL, Jorgensen KM, Soressen E, Thiro L: Charakterisierung des aus Schweineinsulin präparierten Humaninsulin. Aktuel Endokrinol 1981;1:104–114.
28 Chawdhury SA, Dodson EJ, Doson GG, Reynolds DC, Tolley SP, Blundell TL, Cleasby A, Pitty JE, Tickle IJ, Wood SP: The crystal of three nonpancreatic human insulins. Diabetologia 1983;25:460–464.
29 Kern W, Kerner W, Pietrowski R, Fehm HL, Born J: Effects of insulin and hypoglycaemia on the auditory brain stem response in humans. J Neurophysiol 1994;72:678–683.
30 Lewontin R, Fuller C: Genes in the Food: an Exchange. New York Review of Books, June 21, 2001.

evidence that such a threat existed. In a July 1980 news release, for example, the company warned that 'animal insulin could likely be in very short supply in approximately 20 years' [5]. But according to the clinical director of the US National Institute of Arthritis, Diabetes, and Digestive and Kidney Diseases, Dr. Phillip Gordon, the concern over restricted future supplies was 'a smoke screen' [1]. The FDA itself sent mixed signals on the question, with a representative saying that: 'One worries about shortages of animal insulin, though we have not encountered one yet' [1].

Another, and perhaps even more plausible reason for the apparently hasty approval was simple enthusiasm about an exciting new application of recombinant gene technology in medicine.

The fact that some people within the agency may have been uneasy about the hastiness of the review was revealed in 2000 by Henry I. Miller, the medical officer who headed the review in 1982. Miller said that his supervisor had 'refused to sign off on the approval' after such a short review because of concern about what might happen if 'anything goes wrong'. 'When the supervisor went on vacation', Miller [6] wrote, 'I convinced his boss to sign off on the approval'. In fact, Miller's 1982 review included an addendum noting that 'the points raised [by the supervisor] re follow up or additional information on [seven] patients terminated or withdrawn from two of the studies are valid' [7].

The review also noted that Eli Lilly 'is committed – and required – to carry these protocols to their specified time limits, i.e., 24 months as a Phase IV study'. But a mere 6 months later, in March 1983, Eli Lilly told the FDA that it would voluntarily add a warning to the label of Humulin about the possible occurrence of weakened hypoglycemic symptoms in patients transferred from animal insulin. The warning read:

The first symptoms of insulin reaction usually come suddenly and may include fatigue, nervousness or 'shakiness', headache, rapid heartbeat, nausea, and cold sweat.

A few patients who experienced hypoglycemic reactions after being transferred to Humulin have reported that these early warning symptoms were less pronounced than they were with animal-source insulin [8].

In the same year, the FDA approved the label change *and* proceeded to require such a warning on the labels of all 'human' insulins. But why did Eli Lilly make this proposal? 'They knew damn well', a high-ranking FDA scientist told me in 1986 at the FDA's office, which was then located in Rockville, Md.

In the *British National Formulary*, the text describing 'human' insulin hypoglycemia unawareness in 1993 read as follows:

Some patients have reported loss of warning of hypoglycemia after transfer to human insulin. Patients should be warned of this possibility and if they believe that human insulin is responsible for their loss of warning it is reasonable to transfer them back to porcine insulin. When prescribing insulin great care should be taken to specify whether a human or an animal preparation is required. Indications for changing from animal to human preparations must be very carefully considered in the light of these reported problems [9].

By 2006, when 'human' insulin was considered the standard treatment, the text had become shorter:

Some patients have reported loss of hypoglycaemia warning after transfer to human insulin. Clinical studies do not confirm that human insulin decreases hypoglycaemia awareness. If a patient believes that human insulin is responsible for the loss of warning it is reasonable to revert to animal insulin and essential to educate the patient about avoiding hypoglycaemia. Great care should be taken to specify whether a human or an animal preparation is required [10].

A Swiss diabetic who wrote to the IKS[14], the registration agency in her country, about her worrisome experience with 'human' insulin hypoglycemia and the fact that she had not been informed about that risk, received the following answer: 'At the moment, the IKS and its experts do unfortunately not have sufficient proof to request a warning in the package insert'.[15] It was not until 1990 that drug authorities in Germany and Switzerland required that a similar warning be added to the labels of the 'human' insulins produced by Novo Nordisk and Hoechst, the market leaders for insulin in these countries. In the same year, the FDA's Endocrinologic and Metabolic Drugs Advisory Committee held a public hearing on the subject of 'human' insulin hypoglycemia unawareness to which I was invited to speak. Later, the FDA decided to stress the warning on the label by requiring that it be printed in bold letters and be surrounded by a black rectangle, standard practice by the agency for unusually dangerous warnings.

Early Problems with 'Human' Insulin

While most reports of adverse drug events are voluntarily provided to the FDA, all serious, expected adverse drug experiences and all nonserious and unexpected adverse reactions must be reported. Nonetheless, adverse events are significantly underreported: it is estimated that the reports which are submitted to the FDA represent less than 10% of the actual experience. Of the reports in figure 8, 36% of the reactions (with both insulin types) were severe, including 2.6% on animal and 4.3% on 'human' insulin with fatal outcomes. This chart

[14] Interkantonale Kontrollstelle für Heilmittel, registration agency for drugs in Switzerland, today Swissmedic.

[15] Letter from the IKS, Director Dr. J. Pfanner, February 18, 1988.

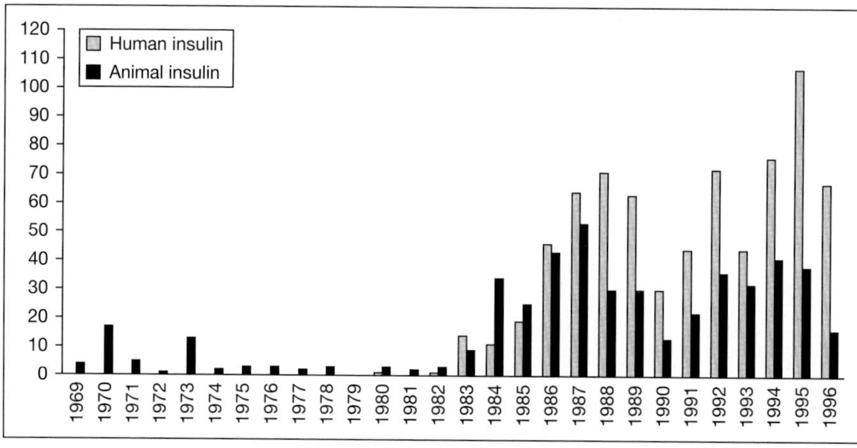

Fig. 8. Hypoglycemia or hypoglycemic reactions reported to the FDA [11].

displays a marked increase in reports during the years after the introduction of 'human' insulin in the United States, due, I believe, to an increased incidence of hypoglycemic unawareness in patients switched to the new products and the consequent loss of glycemic control.

Another foreshadowing of problems with 'human' insulin occurred in a clinical trial performed for Novo at the University of Basel. The study was designed to evaluate 'human' Ultratard and involved 51 insulin-dependent diabetics for the period from September 1983 to November 1984. It concluded that 'human' 'Ultratard is not a suitable basal insulin for type 1 diabetics' [12] since substantial numbers of patients experienced hypoglycemia with diminished warning symptoms. Nevertheless, despite these findings, 'human' Ultratard was licensed in Switzerland on November 30, 1984, possibly before the findings of this study (dated December 1984) were known by the approval authority.

Galloway and Chance [13] (working at the Lilly Research Laboratories) concluded in 1994 after comparing 'human' and animal ultralente that: 'Beef ultralente is more appropriate as a basal insulin, but has the disadvantage of immunogenicity.' This result from laboratory research was confirmed in real-life use: at a postgraduate course organized by the American Diabetes Association in 1995, a physician asked the guest speaker, Dr. D.M. Nathan of the DCCT Research Group, what he recommended when blood sugar levels were not controllable on 'human' ultralente during the night. After Dr. Nathan answered that he used nonhuman NPH for those patients, several physicians emphasized that animal insulin needed to remain available. Dr. Nathan's conclusive statement was:

'I would be unhappy without non-human insulin. I prefer non-human insulin during the night because of smoother control and less hypoglycemia.'[16]

But insulin-dependent diabetics who needed or who preferred animal insulin had the misfortune of being 'directly in the firing line' of recombinant DNA technology, and were targeted as a test of how well such products would be accepted by the market. No one wanted to listen to people who might throw doubts on the new technological revolution.

The insulin industry ignored or discredited reports of serious side effects, and instead aggressively structured its marketing to drive up the sales of what it termed the most human of all insulins. The following advertisement was typical of the link between natural human insulin and the new recombinant DNA insulins (fig. 9).

The number of patients that were transferred to 'human' insulin without medical need caused concern among medical experts, such as Professor Andrew Herxheimer:

'Clinical advantages of human over existing animal insulins have not become apparent over the last 6 years. Prescribers should not change the type or species of insulin without good reason, and then only with the fully informed consent of the patient. I find the lack of symptoms of hypoglycemia worrying especially as regards driving! A general change-over to human insulins is inappropriate' [14].

Even now, major diabetes organizations such as Diabetes UK and the International Diabetes Federation echo Professor Herxheimer's concern:

'Some people are not able to manage their condition effectively with human insulin'.[17]

'There is no overwhelming evidence to prefer one species of insulin over another and patients should not be changed from one species to another without reason' [15].

Early Withdrawal of Animal Insulins

In 1982, Novo planned to replace all their animal insulin in the UK wholesale's repositories with 'human' insulin overnight in a unique action. Thanks to Dr. Laurence Gerlis, at that time Medical Director at Novo UK, who heard of the plan, this was stopped and the exchange was not carried out

[16] Insulin management: what are the options? American Diabetes Association Advanced Postgraduate Course in Endocrinology/Diabetes, DCCT Follow-Up, Boston, January 28–30, 1995 (oral statement).

[17] Diabetes UK, letter to IDDT, February 19, 2004.

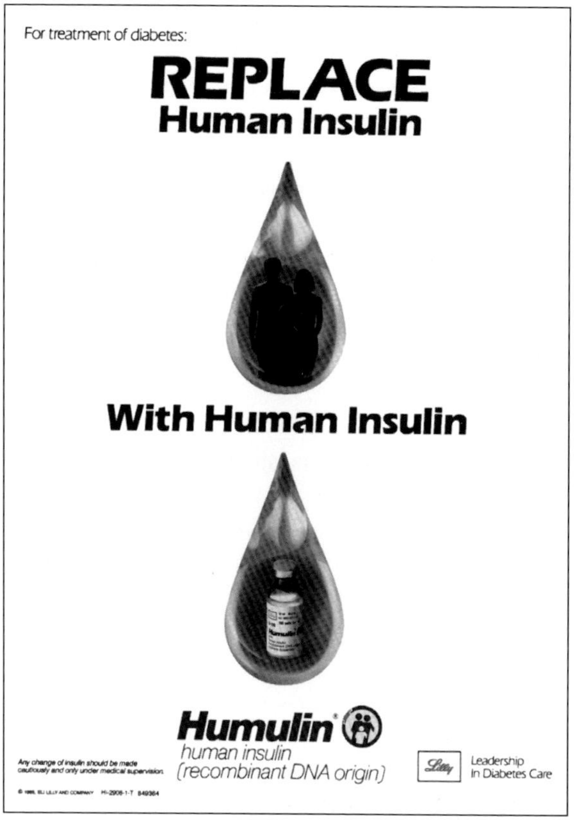

Fig. 9. Advertisement typical of the link between natural human insulin and the new recombinant DNA insulins (1988). Reprinted with permission.

[Dr. Gerlis, pers. commun.]. The UK is today the western European country where animal insulin is used the most, and the only one where it is still produced.

In February 1986, Novo notified major pharmacists in Switzerland that in 5 months the company would withdraw its most popular animal porcine insulins Actrapid MC and Monotard MC, which together composed 70% of the Swiss insulin market. Shortly thereafter, they informed all physicians. Subsequently this decision was 'revised' and those insulins were not withdrawn until 2006. But the damage was done: many physicians, influenced by the company's information, had already changed their patients' therapy to 'human' insulin. Henceforth, rumors of a pending withdrawal would hang over the head of every diabetic and every physician.

One cannot underestimate the impact of Novo's tactic. Once 'human' insulin had achieved a certain market share and was considered by many to be the standard treatment, animal insulins were no longer mentioned in lectures at universities or in the literature about insulin therapy. Indeed, many of today's generation of physicians and patients do not know that there are differences among the insulins.

At the mandatory medical courses – which are often sponsored by insulin producers with free flights and hotels for hundreds of physicians – not only are information and facts conveyed but opinions are formed. Here, the advantages of the latest analogues are put forward and the use of animal insulin is denigrated as a mistake.[18]

Today, the term 'insulin' is assumed to mean 'human' insulin and it has become outdated to speak about the species of insulin. Indeed, most medical research papers on diabetes fail to mention which insulin species has been studied. Worse, studies of insulin analogues use exclusively 'human' insulin as the base comparator.

In 2003, Novo Nordisk changed the names of the 'human' insulins it markets in the UK by omitting the word 'human' from its name. Therefore 'Human Actrapid' became simply 'Actrapid', making it necessary for diabetics using the porcine 'Pork Actrapid', 'Pork Insulatard' and 'Pork Mixtard' to be even more careful about not receiving 'human' insulin by mistake.

Using Insulin Pens as a Marketing Tool

The establishment of intensive insulin therapy – which involves more frequent insulin injections – was facilitated by the introduction of the insulin pen[19]. It soon became very popular, because it enables the diabetic to inject insulin easily, accurately and discretely. Many diabetics soon changed to this alternative to the syringe and were no longer willing to live without such a user-friendly device. When the insulin suppliers provided 'human' insulin in pens, many who did not want to give up the pen were easily switched. The marketing of pens and other devices to patients is not controlled and advertising can be targeted directly at the public, thus stimulating the demand for pens.

In the early 1990s the Pharmacy Department of the University Hospital of Bern noticed that Novo Nordisk's animal insulin now included the notification that the patient could switch to the 'human' variety by using the new insulin pen, thus blurring the line between advertising for the pen and advertising for the insulin.

[18] Professor H. Mehnert at a medical course in Germany, 1998.

[19] A pen is a device for administering insulin injections. Other than the syringe which has to be filled with the appropriate units of insulin from a bottle, pens contain an ampoule filled with insulin and the selected dose can be injected directly.

Shortly after the launch of 'human' insulin, manufacturers stopped providing animal insulin in pens so that patients had to laboriously fill empty pens with the insulin of their choice or go back to using the syringe.

C.H., Retired

C.H., 70, uses a pen with 'human' insulin. As the supplier of this pen only provides 'human' insulin, H. asks whether it would be possible for the company to supply animal insulin in pens as well. He has problems with 'human' insulin, since he does not recognize his hypos in good time. A representative of the pharmaceutical firm Novo Nordisk advises H. to stay with 'human' insulin because it has spread worldwide and is definitely obtainable in many countries. H. feels this 'advice' is improper interference, and so from then on he fills pork insulin into used pen cartridges. When he asks the supplier to put at his disposal at least sterile empty cartridges, they do not respond to his request[pers. commun.].

When animal insulin was no longer available in pens, an organization of Swiss patients[20] tried to find a way for large scale production. There was no way in which they could obtain empty pen cartridges, as they are protected by patents. The Swiss Diabetes Association did not support the project; therefore, the pressure on the manufacturers to provide the pens was undermined, even though the Swiss government concluded that Novo Nordisk abused its leading position in the market in a cartel-like way.

Finally, a solution was found in that the University Hospital of Bern produced pen ampoules with porcine insulin and did so for over 10 years. Novo Nordisk refused to provide empty cartridges, but provided them free filled with physiological salt solution. These were emptied and refilled with porcine insulin in the hospital's pharmacy. In 2004, one cartridge left the pharmacy still filled with salt solution, causing a potentially life-threatening situation. Although no one was hurt, production was stopped immediately, primarily because many of the hospital administrators were certain that 'human' insulin was better.

Thanks to the efforts of advocates of animal insulin, there are currently three animal insulins available in pens in Switzerland: Hypurin porcine neutral, isophane and 30/70 mix. These insulins are manufactured in the UK by Wockhardt and have been registered in Switzerland since 2000.

Many diabetics and their care givers are seduced by the ease with which they can use a ready-filled pen, which is, of course, the goal of the manufacturers. In addition, 'human' insulin is such a part of standard care that people taking part in FIT (Functional Insulin Therapy) courses organized by many Swiss

[20] Patientenvereinigung zur Förderung des natürlichen Insulins PVNI, today Forum Insulin Schweiz FIS (http://www.foruminsulin.ch).

clinics and diabetes associations find that the use of pens – and therefore, almost inevitably, treatment with 'human' insulin – is a requirement.

A Patient's Choice

It is difficult for patients to stand up to physicians even if they do have the right to ask for the medicine they need. At the University Hospital of Bern, a patient's request for animal insulin was refused by a junior doctor and, furthermore, his decision was supported by his superior [pers. commun.]. Patients have at times been forced to change to a different insulin because animal insulin is often not in stock at the hospital's pharmacy and even when patients or their relatives bring their own animal insulin the hospital refuses to use it.

Some physicians simply do not know that animal insulin is available, simply because they do not check. This is a common occurrence, not just in Switzerland but around the world. Physicians either do not know animal insulin is available or they are unwilling to endorse its use to treat insulin-dependent diabetics.

A.W., Occupation Unknown

'After I had been transferred to human insulin about a year ago… I suffered from blackouts… with unusual neuroglycopenic symptoms, which lasted for between 5 to 10 minutes. … During a radio transmission [on "human" insulin hypoglycemia unawareness], my wife noted key sentences that described exactly the symptoms she had seen in me for a year, in very short intervals even during the past few months. In a press conference I attended, my eyes were opened for what I had already been accepting as fate. … I told my doctor about this… He said that the medical professionals had been aware of dangers or disadvantages of human insulins from the beginning, but did override them because of many other, positive attributes. I now use animal Lente insulin again… the described episodes disappeared completely' [pers. commun., 1987].

'Human' insulin became the standard treatment very quickly, before it had been on the market long enough to properly assess its effectiveness. The following story describes the case of a woman who was a victim of this change in 1987.

R.I., Physician's Assistant

'When I was 24 years old, I had severe hyperglycemia with ketoacidosis due to an infection and was admitted to the local hospital. I had been diabetic for 17 years and brought my own porcine insulins to the hospital. Enjoying the luxury of hospital care, I did not prepare the shots myself, but got the syringe already filled.

During my stay at the hospital, I had hypoglycemia in the afternoon twice, without feeling hungry and without trembling, which were my usual warning symptoms for hypoglycemia. The second time I just became very tired and felt so heavy, I could not move my arm to reach the bell and call a nurse. I fell asleep. The nurse had to wake me up, my blood sugar was 3.1 mmol/l. I felt tired as if I had run a long distance. Even eating an apple strained me.

That night, nobody brought me my insulin. I asked the nurse and went to the medicine cupboard to get it myself. Everything was ready, my name was written on the syringe and the vial, only it was not the insulin I had brought to the hospital, but "human" insulin. The hospital staff had changed my insulin without even telling me. When I asked the hospital physician, he only told me this insulin was like my normal insulin' [pers. commun.].

Such changes of insulin without warning occurred not only in Switzerland, but throughout western Europe and North America. The BDA deplored the fact that the therapy of some people had been changed without their knowledge or consent.

Withdrawals Continue

Today, not only animal insulins, but also the first generation of 'human' insulins are being withdrawn from the market. The timing is no coincidence: The patents covering those insulins are running out, making it possible for other manufacturers to produce generic products and sell them cheaper than the originals. When the original products are withdrawn, patients are forced to change to analogue insulins before a new supplier may offer a generic product. Since changing insulin is not attractive to patients, most of them would not change back after a year or two, even if there were a manufacturer willing to produce the generic product for a destroyed market.

In an ongoing promotion campaign in Switzerland, the manufacturer of the insulin pens for Lantus[21] explains the success of this insulin by the fact that it is the only long-acting insulin available. What the campaign does not say is that bovine, porcine and 'human' insulins with stable kinetics of 24 h and more have been withdrawn. In fact, beef ultralente insulin, long considered the most stable basal insulin, with a duration of up to 36 h, was the first animal variety to be withdrawn from the North American market.

In 2006, G-BA[22], Germany's health insurance governing body, decided that short-acting analogues for type 2 diabetics would not be paid for by the public

[21] Insulin analogue, generic name insulin glargin, with intermediate kinetics of 24 h.

[22] Gemeinsamer Bundesausschuss: A medical self-governing body, formed by the national associations of doctors and dentists, the German Hospital Federation and the healthy insurance funds, gives concrete definition to the legal requirements created by the Legislature and implements them.

health insurance system unless the manufacturer lowered its prices by 30–60% to match the cost of 'human' insulin. This decision caused an outcry in the diabetic community, because patients were afraid that the products they wanted would no longer be available. The report of the IQWiG[23] on the use of short acting analogues in type 1 diabetes concluded that advantages over 'human' insulin were not supported by sufficient evidence [16].

Novo Nordisk, the market leader in insulins in Europe, declared in 2006 that it would in future produce only analogue insulins and initiate the withdrawal of all of its currently available 'human' insulins in 2008.[24] This means that in due course 16,000 patients in the UK will no longer be able to obtain their current insulin products and will have to switch to more expensive analogues. Novo Nordisk declared that 'withdrawing old insulins will allow us to concentrate our future investment in research in more advanced therapy for the benefit of people with diabetes' [17]. In the long term, it appears that the discussion as to whether or not analogues should be funded by the health insurance system will be decided by the industry. This is a public policy decision that only diabetics themselves may be able to change.

Insulin for the World's Poorest Countries

In 2001, the health department of Togo announced a change from animal to 'human' insulin. The arguments they used for this a change were the same spurious arguments that had proved so successful elsewhere, i.e. that 'human' insulin is purer and more physiologically appropriate. Animal insulins in Togo used to be sold in U40[25] concentrations, whereas 'human' insulins are U100. Therefore there are two types of syringes, one for each concentration, with the result that one type of insulin might be put in the syringe for the other type; consequently there is a risk of injecting too much or not enough insulin. This was the official reason why animal insulins were declared illegal in Togo, even though there are U100 animal insulins available and other countries worldwide use the two concentrations simultaneously. Other African countries followed the lead of Togo, with the consequence that animal insulin is also banned from Senegal and Burundi.

[23] Institut für Qualität und Wirtschaftlichkeit im Gesundheitswesen: Institute that evaluates the quality and efficiency of health care, in this case providing the basis for decision making to the G-BA.

[24] Letter from Viggo L. Birch to Jenny Hirst (President of the IDDT), August 2, 2006.

[25] 40 IU/ml.

It has to be mentioned that in sub-Saharan countries, prices for 'human' insulins are between 3 and 10 times higher than for animal insulins. Some insulin manufacturers do for a time offer a discount to governments in order to introduce 'human' insulins, which may not be fully passed on to the patient.

There is still the promise that technical advances will make 'human' insulin cheaper to produce, but the significant cost savings of this method of production, in use since the early 1980s, have not yet been passed on to patients. After 20 years, no considerable price reduction has occurred; in fact, the exact opposite has taken place. Each new insulin analogue is progressively more expensive than the one which came before, and these were more expensive than the first line of recombinant DNA insulins introduced in the 1980s. It seems that the pharmaceutical industry is more interested in developing new analogues than in finding cheaper production methods. If the prices of 'human' insulins did fall, this would be because of competition from generic producers and not because of reduced production costs. One should not forget that the charge made for insulins does not have to cover production costs alone, but also has to cover distribution, marketing and research as well as the costs associated with regulatory approval. All of these factors are not affected by lower production costs.

One example of a successful venture to make insulin more available in a developing country is a project initiated at my suggestion in 1994 by the Swiss Tropical Institute and the Foundation for Diabetes and Nutrition in Dar es Salaam, Tanzania.[26] The aim of the project is to improve the quality of life and life expectancy of patients with diabetes in an economically sustainable way. To achieve this goal, health staff were trained at three municipal hospitals, so that diabetes health care could be decentralized. The insulin selected was cost-effective animal insulin bought at the market price. Cost sharing was introduced to cover the cost of the medicine, with patients contributing 20% of the cost each year. In 7 years, the number of patients included in the project rose from 450 to over 5,500, 30% of them insulin-dependent type 1 diabetics. Even though 11% were unable to pay for drugs, patients contributed 50% to the overall cost of insulin. The other 50% was paid by the World Bank through the Tanzanian health department in order to sustain the project and in recognition of the high level of patient participation. Serious hypoglycemia was reported in 1.5 patients/month, while at the national referring hospital Muhimbili, where

[26] Wiedenmayer K, Mtasiwa D, Teuscher A: Selecting natural animal insulin improves access to cost-effective therapy of diabetic patients in the public sector of Dar es Salaam, Tanzania. Poster presentation at the 40th Annual European Diabetes and Epidemiology Group (EDEG) Meeting, Siófok, Hungary, April 2–5, 2005.

patients are provided with 'human' insulin, hypoglycemia was reported in 3 patients/month in 2002.

In conclusion, it can be said that diabetes therapy can be optimized by selecting cost-effective animal insulin, life expectancy and quality of life can be improved with decentralized provision of animal insulin and cost sharing at affordable levels. However, an adequate range of animal insulins must be available internationally to achieve these objectives.

References

1 As Lilly's synthetic insulin gets FDA OK, Novo, Biogen join to clone their own. Biotechnology Newswatch, Nov 15, 1982.

2 Marples A: Ironman/diabetic. Eli Lilly advertisement. Diabetes Dialogue, May/June/July 1986.

3 Sylvester R: Doctors attack 'inferior' NHS human insulin. The Sunday Telegraph, Jan 22, 1995.

4 Owens DR, Zinman B, Bolli GB: Insulins today and beyond. Lancet 2001;358:739–746.

5 Eli Lilly: News release. PR Newswire, July 21, 1980.

6 Miller HI: To America's Health: a Proposal to Reform the Food and Drug Administration. Stanford, Hoover Institution Press, Stanford University, 2000, pp 41–42.

7 US Food and Drug Administration: NDA 18,780 and 18,781, Medical Officers' Review (MOR) of New Drug Application (NDA), July 20, 1982.

8 Physician's Desk Reference: Product information: Humulin. Oradell, Medical Economics, 1987, pp 1142–1144.

9 BNF (British National Formulary), No 25. British Medical Association and The Royal Pharmaceutical Society of Great Britain, London, March 1993, p 255.

10 BNF (British National Formulary), No 52. September 2006, online edition http://www.bnf.org/bnf/bnf/current/4081.htm (13.3.2007).

11 Annual Adverse Drug Experience Reports, Surveillance and Data Processing Branch, Division of Pharmacovigilance and Epidemiology Office of Epidemiology and Biostatistics Center for Drug Evaluation and Research. US Food and Drug Administration, 1969–1996.

12 Berger W, Pasquel M: Schlussbericht über die klinische Erfahrung mit dem Humaninsulinpräparat 'Ultratard', Dec 1984. Data on file Novo.

13 Galloway JA, Chance RE: Improving insulin therapy: achievements and challenges. Horm Metab Res 1994;26:591–598.

14 Herxheimer A: Human insulins: an update. Drug Ther Bull 1989;27:21–24.

15 International Diabetes Federation: Position Statement: Animal, Human and Analogue Insulins, March 2005. http://www.idf.org/home/index.cfm?node = 1385. 1.3.2007.

16 Institut für Qualität und Wirtschaftlichkeit im Gesundheitswesen: Kurzwirksame Insulinanaloga zur Behandlung des Diabetes mellitus Typ. 1. Abschlussbericht A05-02. Köln:IQWiG;2007.

17 Birch VL (Vice President Europe North): Novo Nordisk insulin discontinuation information: an open letter from Novo Nordisk to all nurses in the United Kingdom. J Diabetes Nurs, June 2005.

Advocacy

by Jenny Hirst

In the early 1980s when 'human' insulin was first introduced, patient advocacy was almost unheard of. Historically and culturally patients respected their doctors. They believed that the doctor knew best and assumed that they were receiving treatment that was in their best interests. Their role was that of the compliant patient, although perhaps they would not have recognized this description of themselves. By today's standards, most patients were naïve.

The concept that treatment decisions should be based on the evidence presented in systematic reviews of randomized controlled trials was simply not in the public domain. The pharmaceutical industry was not as powerful and influential as it has become and generally patients were unaware of any possible influences industry may have had on doctors, health professionals, patients' organizations or, indeed, of the close relationship of the industry with regulatory authorities. Prior to the introduction of 'human' insulin, drugs were chemical in origin and adverse reactions were more predictable. Overall doctors appeared to respect patients' reports about adverse reactions and would prescribe an alternative drug. The introduction of 'human' insulin in 1982 and lack of action take on subsequent reports of adverse reactions changed many patients' perspectives forever and in the world of diabetes, patient advocacy began.

In the UK the British Diabetic Association (BDA) as it was then known, now Diabetes UK, was the only charity for diabetes and when it was founded in 1934, it was the first charitable organization to formally include both patients and doctors within a single organization. This was recognized as a major step forward: people living with diabetes and doctors jointly addressing issues of common concern. But was this an equal partnership and were the nonmedical members the first patient advocates? In the 1980s, it became obvious to some activists in the BDA that this partnership was far from equal, something that was highlighted by the 'human' and animal insulin debate. When the BDA received complaints of adverse reactions to 'human' insulin but took little action, people living with diabetes had opposing views to many of the doctors within the organization. It was clear that if people with diabetes were to be actively involved in their own care and if they were to have a choice of insulin treatment, patient advocacy would be essential.

Reports of Adverse Reactions

During the mid- to late 1980s the BDA received nearly 3,000 adverse reaction reports from people who had been transferred from beef or pork insulin to 'human' insulin. Often this transfer had taken place without their knowledge as pharmacies simply replaced patients' usual animal insulin with 'human' insulin. We may never know whether this reflected assumptions that 'human' was identical to animal insulin, a lack of respect for patients being involved in decisions about their treatment, the influence of the pharmaceutical industry in marketing their latest product, or all three.

Initially the most common complaint was a loss of the warning symptoms of hypoglycemia resulting in comas with or without seizures and subsequent increase in the number of hypoglycemic events. Yet despite the similarity of the adverse reactions in people from all over the UK, these complaints were largely ignored by the BDA and many physicians. People were told it was 'all in your imagination' or it was simply a matter of a 'slight dose adjustment'. Arguably, the most damaging reaction was the refusal by many doctors to change people back to the animal insulin that had previously suited them, as demonstrated by a statement by a patient, quoted in an unpublished report of Dr. Natasha Posner commissioned by the BDA in 1992:

'My consultant was unsympathetic and made me feel inadequate and stupid, rapidly diminishing my confidence and, in fact, aggravating my condition through stress.'

This approach damaged the doctor/patient relationship and made patients suspicious and less trusting. In reality patients who had been transferred from animal insulin to 'human' insulin were part of an 'unofficial' large-scale trial not just of 'human' insulin but of the first genetically produced drug to be approved for use in man. This group was in an ideal position to compare the effects of both insulins and yet their reports of adverse reactions to 'human' insulin were largely dismissed as merely anecdotal and of little relevance. Some patients and their family carers knew that hypoglycemic warning symptoms were less pronounced with 'human' insulin, so why did doctors ignore their reports and not take the obvious action of returning them to animal insulin? Why did doctors representing the BDA publicly deny that 'human' insulin caused adverse reactions in some people? Above all, why was 'human' insulin assumed to be better when there was no evidence to support this?

Reactions of People with Diabetes

This situation led to anger, frustration and suspicion that the pharmaceutical industry was influencing doctors and treatment choices, all of which contributed to patient advocacy as we now know it in the UK. But perhaps above all, the driving force was fear – fear that their previously healthy life when using animal insulin had come to an end, fear about the loss of their quality of life and fear that for the rest of their life they were going to be faced with adverse reactions, including hypoglycemia without warning symptoms and its ensuing dangers.

In 1991 a group of 700 patients [1] and their family carers attempted to take legal action against the insulin manufacturers but failed for a lack of scientific evidence to support their adverse experiences. With hind sight, we know that this lack of scientific evidence was a case of *'absence of evidence'* not *'evidence of absence'* of side effects. This was because no large-scale, long-term trials had been carried out to provide such evidence. Patient advocates were fighting an uphill battle against the pharmaceutical companies and the medical profession who had more expertise and financial support than they had.

Protracted patient advocacy continued within the BDA and in the early 1990s the association commissioned Dr. Natasha Posner to carry out a study of the reports about adverse reactions with the stated intention of submitting the report for publication in the *British Medical Journal*. However, the report was never submitted because the BDA considered it was 'too alarmist'. This failure to accept that people with diabetes not only needed but had a right to know the truth about the effects of 'human' insulin resulted in the formation of a separate organization, the Insulin Dependent Diabetes Trust (IDDT) – a patient/carer advocacy group.

The Formation of the Insulin Dependent Diabetes Trust (IDDT), 1994

The first board of trustees of the IDDT was made up of 6 people including 2 doctors prepared to support the patients – Dr. Matthew Kiln, a physician with type 1 diabetes who was unable to tolerate 'human' insulin and Dr. Laurence Gerlis who was director of medical research for the insulin manufacturer Novo at the time 'human' insulin was introduced.

The aims of IDDT were clear and remain the same today:

- To offer care and support to people with diabetes and their carers, especially those experiencing difficulties with synthetic 'human' insulin.
- To influence appropriate government bodies to ensure that a wide range of insulins, including animal insulins, remains available to suit the needs of all insulin users.
- To ensure that patients and carers have an *informed* choice of insulin treatment.

The trustees made two significant decisions from the outset that hold true today. Firs, IDDT would not accept pharmaceutical industry funding in order to be and be seen to be totally independent and uninfluenced. Second, IDDT would not be involved in any form of litigation as its priority had to be to try to safeguard future supplies of animal insulins rather than to seek financial compensation for people adversely affected by 'human' insulin.

Adverse Reactions

IDDT's first task was to collect information from people with diabetes and family carers about their experiences with 'human' insulin. Questionnaires were sent to everyone who contacted IDDT and an analysis showed that on average the adverse effects did not appear until 13 months after treatment with 'human' insulin began. Most people complained of 3 or 4 of the following adverse reactions:

- 41% – loss of warnings of hypos or 'I function on automatic pilot'
- 34% – extreme tiredness or lethargy
- 9% – sleeping all the time
- 32% – weight increase of 1.5 stones (21 pounds) and more
- 28% – feeling unwell all the time
- 24% – memory loss or confusion
- 9% – blood glucose levels dipping and peaking erratically
- 8% – described by their families as 'not the same person'
- 5% – mood changes, described as difficult to live with
- 7% – pains, especially in the legs and joints
- 4% – irregular or late menstrual periods.

It became the major role of the IDDT to provide correct information about the availability status of animal insulins despite information to the contrary from health professionals. Almost by definition this also meant encouraging people to be assertive with their doctors and health professionals and to insist on having the animal insulin they felt suited them best.

The second task the IDDT took on was to gather evidence from independent sources. They found that Herxheimer in the *Drug and Therapeutics Bulletin* [2] and the *British National Formulary* [3] advised that 'human' insulin had no advantages over conventional insulins. They also recognized that patients' experiences of loss of the warning symptoms of hypoglycemia were valid, advising that 'if (patients) believe that human insulin is responsible for their loss of warnings it is reasonable to transfer them back to porcine insulins'. This reputable evidence gave confidence to patients who, for the first time, felt able to exercise their right to choose their treatment in the diabetes clinic setting.

The Bellagio Report 1996

Being aware of Professor Teuscher's published studies on 'human' insulin, IDDT recognized that he was one of the very few physicians who had listened to his patients and had bravely and openly expressed concerns about 'human' insulin. The IDDT decided to contact him which resulted in a team residency which was supported by the Rockefeller Foundation, New York, N.Y., and held at the Foundation's Study and Conference Center in Bellagio, Italy. The team consisted of physicians and scientists from both developed and developing countries and patients and family carers who met to formulate their joint needs with respect to 'human' and animal insulins. This was probably the first time that such a group had worked together as equal partners with mutual respect and resulted in the publication of the Bellagio Report.

The Bellagio Report recognized that the welfare of people with diabetes is dependent on their active participation in their care and this can only be achieved if they are able to make an informed choice about their treatment, including risks and benefits of all insulin treatment options. This was a radical statement in 1996 as then the idea of patient involvement in their own care was little more than a germinating seed. The report drew attention to the lack of evidence of benefit of 'human' insulin but also to the neurophysiological differences during hypoglycemia with 'human' and animal insulins which offered an explanation for the loss of 'hypo' warnings with 'human' insulin. It made recommendations that animal insulins should be available in all countries and that they should be the first-line treatment for all those for whom hypoglycemia may be of special concern, especially people in developing countries who have little or no access to blood glucose monitoring.

IDDT published the Bellagio Report and circulated it to all diabetes associations and health ministries around the world and in 2007 it is still quoted by people who access it via the internet. Patient advocates learned a very important lesson: the value of searching the literature so that advocacy can be based on evidence and the importance of the absence of evidence as a result of research not being carried out.

The Value of Evidence and Putting It to Good Use

Thanks to Sir Iain Chalmers, then head of the Cochrane Collaboration in Oxford, IDDT became involved in the Cochrane Diabetes and Endocrinology Group from which it learned to look at research differently – its quality, methodology and its independence (or otherwise) from industry. In 2002, the Cochrane Review comparing 'human' and animal insulin was published [4] and showed no clinically relevant differences. However, it also showed that many patient-oriented outcomes were never investigated in high-quality randomized clinical trials, such as diabetes complication and mortality rates and health-related quality of life – all important issues for patients. As advocates had suspected, 'human' insulin was introduced without sufficient proof of its advantages and safety. This was a key development for patients who now had even more evidence to support their wishes to change back to animal insulin.

The International Perspective

During this time IDDT was acutely aware that there could be other people suffering from similar symptoms without realizing that the cause could be 'human' insulin; therefore, steps were taken to reach other people with diabetes by developing a website and contacting journalists. Both steps had an amazing effect and the IDDT membership grew with people reporting the same adverse experiences and the same misinformation but they also expressed relief that they were not alone and that there was an organization that was fighting for the continued availability of animal insulins. It also became clear that this was not an issue that only affected people in the UK and Switzerland. People from countries around the world reported similar adverse reactions to 'human' insulins and some had already formed advocacy groups. In 1998, an umbrella organization, IDDT-International, was launched with representative groups in Australia, Canada, Germany, Switzerland and the United States enabling advocates in the different countries to share information and work together towards a common goal. In addition, the Society for Diabetic Rights (SDR) was formed in Canada with similar aims to IDDT-Canada but with the intention of exploring litigation.

Lobbying

With the support of significant numbers of people in need of animal insulins with case histories showing the adverse effects of 'human' insulin and the scientific evidence, the international groups lobbied their respective governments. IDDT and its members wrote countless letters to UK government departments and to Members of Parliament (MPs) but the response was always predictable: 'we continue to monitor the safety of "human" insulin' and 'government cannot interfere with the commercial decisions of pharmaceutical companies'.

However, our case received support from many MPs who understood that all drugs can cause adverse reactions in some people and they, in turn, raised key issues with the Minister of Health. These issues included: (1) the increased cost to the public purse by first-line use of the more expensive 'human' insulin despite its unproven superiority and (2) the question why the National Institute for Clinical Excellence (NICE) has not assessed all insulins and issued guidance for their use, as with many other drugs.

After 11 years, success came in 2005 when the then Minister of Health, Jane Kennedy, stated[27]:

'The Department of Health fully accepts that some people are better suited to animal insulins and they should continue to be available'.

Similarly in Canada, thanks to the lobbying of the Society for Diabetics Rights (SDR), Ms. Julia Hill of the Ministry of Health stated to the House of Commons Standing Committee on Health in 2003:

'...our first statement is that there very clearly are Canadians who need animal-sourced insulins to manage their diabetes. We have no doubt about that at all'[28].

This acceptance by two governments might appear to be the end of the story, but sadly it is not. The two major global animal insulin manufacturers, Eli Lilly and Novo Nordisk, systematically started to discontinue all their animal insulins and by the end of 2007 this global discontinuation will be complete. This leaves people in many countries in the position of having to go through lengthy and expensive personal importation processes to obtain the animal insulins they need. The UK is in the fortunate position of having a second supplier, Wockhardt UK (formerly CP Pharmaceuticals), but having only one small supplier with a history of supply problems puts people in a very vulnerable position.

What Has Our Advocacy Achieved?

- We have kept animal insulin available for 20 years longer than intended by the manufacturers and people like my daughter have been able to remain healthy for a further 20 years.
- IDDT and the international groups have been contacted by several thousand people and made them aware that an animal insulin option is available. As a result many have reported improvements in their health and quality of life; this is by far the most important achievement.
- Despite criticisms from many quarters, advocates of insulin choice and the continued availability of animal insulins have kept this issue alive within the diabetes community, in health ministries, regulatory bodies, national diabetes associations and the media.

[27] Letter from Jane Kennedy to IDDT.

[28] Oral statement, Standing Committee on Health, 37th Parliament, 2nd Session, February 3, 2003.

- In the UK the Department of Health has declared that some people need animal insulin and that it should continue to be available. The Minister of Health has referred to an 'Insulin Strategy' whereby future supplies of animal insulins are to be secured.
- Joint advocacy by IDDT-Canada and the Society for Diabetic Rights (SDR) resulted in Health Canada inviting Wockhardt UK to apply for marketing authorization for pork insulin and in April 2006, it became available in Canada, though at a very high price. Follow-up meetings are taking place and at the time of writing, Health Canada is inviting an insulin producer in Argentina to apply for approval to market both beef and pork insulins in Canada.
- Advocacy in Australia has resulted in special arrangements being made whereby pork insulin will be available by special access from a local distributor in Australia, thereby cutting down costs and transportation problems due to high temperatures. Pork insulin was discontinued in Australia at the end of the 1980s within a very short period of time with little or no warning to patients. Correspondence on file with the President of Diabetes Australia (July 1990) demonstrates that this arrangement had been approved by the government and the pharmaceutical industry.
- In Germany, 150 people are importing pork insulin from Argentina and other countries are likely to follow suit as this source is cheaper than importing it from the UK.

The clear message from our achievements is that people with diabetes will fight for the insulin they need to remain healthy and, in some cases, even alive. In the Journal of the International Diabetes Federation, the then President, Professor Sir George Alberti, wrote:

'Personally I care less about what sort of insulin is available, and more about that it is accessible, affordable, of reasonable quality – and works' [5].

However, patient advocates do care about what sort of insulin is available – all types of insulin must be available to suit the varying needs of everyone with diabetes. Animal insulin is essential in the developed world for people unable to tolerate synthetic insulins but it is also essential for people in developing countries because it works, it is significantly more affordable for poor people and it saves more lives.

The Role of the Pharmaceutical Industry

The story of 'human' insulin cannot be written without mentioning the huge role the pharmaceutical industry played. As we have already read, the very name 'human' insulin was a marketing ploy that certainly misled patients and perhaps even health professionals. The claims that 'human' insulin was superior to animal insulins were not based on evidence from good quality research. Industry's marketing techniques effectively forced patients to change to 'human' insulin and in the UK they succeeded with over 84% of patients being transferred for commercial and not clinical reasons.

Industry's close relationship with national diabetes associations and years of undeclared funding give rise to questions about influence, as does their close relationship with regulatory bodies and, of course, with members of the medical profession.

Perhaps the greatest criticism of the industry and all those involved in what can be described as one of the largest untold medical scandals is that the pharmaceutical companies ignored the reports of patients. They failed to listen, they failed to carry out research to gauge the magnitude of the problem and they failed to assess the long-term safety of the first genetically produced drug to be prescribed to humans. As advocates we recognize that the duty of pharmaceutical companies is primarily to their shareholders but they do have a moral duty to show respect and care for the consumers of their products – people with diabetes.

And the Future...

In the late 1990s insulin analogues were introduced. Within months of their introduction, IDDT started to receive adverse reaction reports not only from people who had been using animal insulin but also from those who previously had been happy with 'human' insulin. It was almost a repeat performance of the introduction of 'human' insulin, but this time IDDT and other advocates were more experienced. We recognized the manufacturers' marketing techniques of referring to them as 'designer insulins' or 'modern insulins' – sounds good but has little meaning, is quite unscientific in not describing the type of insulin and certainly does not mean that they are superior to other insulins. We looked at the evidence with greater experience and found that analogues have little benefit for the majority of people.

A Cochrane Review [6] of short-acting insulin analogues again concluded that the majority of studies were methodologically poor with over 80% of them funded by the manufacturers and no funding sources declared for the remaining studies. This time we recognized that this was hardly independent, reliable research on which patients and doctors should make treatment changes. Yet despite this, the very significantly more expensive insulin analogues are taking over as a first-line treatment. At a time when the UK National Health Service limits the costs of drugs, serious questions must be raised about the logic of changing people to highly expensive insulin analogues that have little proven benefit and unknown long-term safety implications. Is this another triumph of marketing over science?

It is of great concern to the IDDT and others that not only has the long-term safety of insulin analogues not been established but that they have the potential for carcinogenic effects. There is increasing evidence to justify these concerns [7]. Even the Position Statement [8] on insulins by the International Diabetes Federation, which is very reliant on pharmaceutical industry funding, concluded that:

'Newer insulins offer potential advantages but until these are proven to deliver real long-term benefits safely and affordably, it seems appropriate to use them in patients experiencing specific problems that a specific analogue might reasonably be expected to address'.

However, these concerns have little effect on the commercial policies of pharmaceutical companies and in 2006 Novo Nordisk stated that they are globally discontinuing 'human' insulins and 'converting the market' to analogue insulins. This 'one type of insulin fits all' approach is wrong and will undoubtedly harm some patients but discontinuations have already begun reducing the range of insulin choices even further so that only insulins with unknown long-term safety and carcinogenic risks remain widely available.

So what does the future hold for patient advocates? We have learned that sheer determination and refusal to give up can bring dividends – animal insulin is still available, albeit from different sources and by different means, and sometimes at greater cost. We will continue with the same determination to try to ensure that people with diabetes, both now and in the future, have an informed choice of safe, affordable insulins to suit all their varying needs. When health and even lives are at stake, this really is a case of having no other choice.

References

1 BMJ Editors' Choice. BMJ, Sep 14, 1991, vol 303.

2 Herxheimer A: Human insulins: an update. Drug Ther Bull 1989;27:21–24.

3 BNF (British National Formulary), No 30. British Medical Association and The Royal Pharmaceutical Society of Great Britain, London, September 1995.

4 Richter B, Neises G: 'Human' insulin versus animal insulin in people with diabetes mellitus. Cochrane Library, 2002. http://www.cochrane.org.

5 Alberti G: Addressing the insulin challenges. Diabetes Voice 2002;47:4.

6 Siebenhofer A, Plank J, Berghold A, et al: Short acting insulin analogues versus regular human insulin in patients with diabetes mellitus. Cochrane Library, 2004. http://www.cochrane.org.

7 Eckardt K, May C, Koenen M, Eckel J: Enhanced mitogenic potency of insulin analogs in human fibroblasts and smooth muscle cells is mediated by IGF-I receptor signaling. Diabetes 2006;55(suppl 1):463.

8 International Diabetes Federation website: http://www.idf.org/home/index.cfm?node = 5 1.2.2007.

Outlook and Recommendations

This book represents a review of the debate, now more than 20 years old, about animal and 'human' insulin. We have told the story from the time when animal insulin was first used in Canada until the achievement of a marked improvement in quality and the subsequent efforts by the diabetes industry to expand its markets with new patented insulin brands. The most notable of these was the introduction of what is called 'human' insulin, a misnomer permitted by the FDA and other regulatory authorities despite the fact that it was by no means human. The name merely served to mislead people with diabetes and to suggest benefits that have remained unproven.

Such maneuvers, coupled with a mass withdrawal of animal insulin, helped ensure that 'human' insulins and later analogues would become the first line of treatment for newly diagnosed diabetic patients.

Indeed, insulin withdrawals have played a key role in strategies to shift insulin users from animal to patented brands. The lente insulins – semilente, lente, ultralente – have long been considered a highly desirable therapy because of their quality and long action but were among the first animal insulins to be withdrawn. I consider semilente insulin, in particular, to be one of the best insulins available because of its reliability. With others in Switzerland I have expressed my concerns about Novo Nordisk's stated intention to withdraw its semilente product from the Swiss market. The company has responded negatively to requests to keep their semilente insulin available and withdrew the product from the Swiss and German market in May 2007. It is possible to obtain semilente from Poland or other Eastern European countries, but we do face the same problem of unreliable supplies currently faced by people in the UK and Canada described above.

Animal insulin from Eastern Europe, South America and developing countries are of a high quality but often little is known about where it actually comes from. This, of course, reflects the general problem of a lack of transparency and secrecy endemic in the drug industry. Physicians and diabetic patients not only lack information about the origin of pharmaceutical products but also have no idea of the marketing strategy employed by manufacturers until they are affected by it. Unless laws are changed to make the industry more transparent and accountable to the public, it is not likely that this situation will improve.

Corporate plans for the insulin market have met with mounting resistance around the world. Beginning in the 1990s, people with diabetes began linking arms to fight for ongoing access to animal insulin. A significant focus of these groups has been the quality and integrity of the scientific evidence. These voices have played a critical role in maintaining access and in exposing the questionable marketing tactics of the insulin monopolies. Activists have proven to be courageous, compassionate, and tireless in their evidence-based campaigns for animal insulin and, equally important, for the right of informed choice.

But now the question is, 'Where do we go from here?' How can we assure that every person who requires insulin is able to exercise the 'right of informed choice'?

The objectives of the worldwide movement to protect and enhance access to natural animal insulin must identify and support a common program. There is an emerging consensus about specific objectives shared among organized diabetics, their families and physicians in a number of countries which include:

- Recognition by health regulators and medical professionals that 'human' insulin is not suitable for all patients
- A strategy to support 'insulin choice' among patients, including animal insulin
- Safe and reliable sources for bovine and porcine pancreases
- Access to beef and pork insulin at affordable prices and inclusion of these insulins in national or subnational formularies

In a few countries, patients' activities have achieved a number of these goals, but nowhere have all these issues been won. It will take an international effort to move this modest agenda forward.

As this book goes to print, we are at a turning point in the 25 years since recombinant DNA technology brought seismic changes to the global insulin market. It seems to me that under the present circumstances the only way to maintain the supply of animal insulin is through advocacy. In addition to advocacy, the persistent efforts of those members of the medical profession who share our concerns are essential. One example of effective international advocacy occurred in 2002 when an international group led by activists from the UK and Switzerland requested that the World Health Organization add semilente insulin to its list of essential medicines.[29] While insulin is listed as an essential medicine, our goal of a distinct listing for animal insulin was not achieved

[29] WHO Model List of Essential Medicines. The list is updated every 2 years by the World Health Organization and is available online at http://www.who.int/medicines/publications/essentialmedicines/en/.

at that time. Nonetheless, even simply raising the issue in such a large forum helped our cause because it raised awareness about the need for animal insulin.

If manufacturers succeed in their campaign to eliminate animal insulin from the world market many will suffer, and not just those who require this kind of insulin to survive. The precedent that was set by the withdrawal of most of the world's animal insulin is now being felt by users of 'human' insulin as well. Animal insulin was the first casualty of the big insulin producers who dominate the market around the world, but they are not the last. As Jenny Hirst so well put it in the chapter on Advocacy, the introduction of insulin analogues 'was almost a repeat performance of the introduction of "human" insulin', including the pattern of insulin withdrawals. Already patients who successfully manage their diabetes with 'human' insulin are now facing the very real dilemma of products being withdrawn when their patents have expired, only to be replaced by insulin analogues.

Advocacy groups across the world are working hard to ensure this never happens. In a growing number of countries, in particular the UK, Canada and more recently Australia, significant progress has been made to safeguard access to animal insulin. Increasingly, they are linking arms across international boundaries, sharing tactics and strategies, evidence and experience. They have also joined a growing community of consumers, medical practitioners, health professionals, scientists and researchers to curb the power and influence of the pharmaceutical industry and hold it to account. These diabetes activists are pragmatic and, most importantly, independent of pharmaceutical manufacturers.

The diabetes industry – composed of insulin manufacturers as well as companies that market insulin pumps, glucose meters and test strips, oral medications, syringes, pens and even insurers – are a formidable force to be reckoned with. That is why, in the future, advocates and activists campaigning for animal insulin will have to coordinate their strategies and stand shoulder to shoulder.

Every country is different, and national strategies will have to take local cultural and regulatory realities on board. International leadership will depend on strong and vigorous national campaigns. The IDDT has affiliates in a number of countries, and during the past 13 years has developed a great deal of expertise both in the UK and internationally. It is well positioned to speak on behalf of people who need and want animal insulin. It is important that this movement matures and, as an international 'umbrella', effectively and vigorously advances the interests of insulin users.

Organizing patients to support access to safe, effective insulin is no easy task. We are hampered by a lack of funds, by the lack of transparency regarding clinical studies, and by the growing distance between ourselves and the evidence which, 20 years ago, was able to shed light on the experiences of many patients. We must continue to insist on the use of the best evidence, but we must also challenge the objectivity of industry-sponsored clinical trials and the lack of transparency which currently characterizes such studies.

The global insulin market is in the throes of change and restructuring. Eli Lilly and Novo Nordisk have for many years dominated the world market, but new players are now aggressively pushing for a piece of the very large and growing pie. Efforts are underway to 'grow' insulin on genetically modified safflower plants, while generic manufacturers are hoping to produce 'human' insulin and sell it less expensively. The ability of people in developing countries to obtain safe, effective and affordable insulin is of rising concern. The incidence of type 2 diabetes is alarming health officials around the world, while the diabetes industry is primarily concerned with how to capture this growing revenue stream. Insulin is heavily promoted as an early treatment for patients with type 2 diabetes, sometimes replacing diet, exercise and even oral medications.

While there are several companies producing safe animal insulin, they are relatively small and the availability of their products is not as reliable as it needs to be. In addition, more than one independent producer of high-quality animal insulin has been taken over by a large multinational company. This has resulted in an abrupt halt to the production of the natural product, part of the very deliberate campaign by these global pharmaceuticals to limit patient choice to the more lucrative 'human' insulin and thereby boost profits.

Access to needed medicines is a global challenge. One example of a successful effort to provide drugs to patients who need them but who lack access is the Roll Back Malaria program run by the African Medical & Research Foundation (AMREF) with the support of several international agencies and private foundations.[30] Despite the overwhelming need for effective antimalarial strategies, including vaccines, pharmaceutical manufacturers made little effort to respond because they felt that the market was too weak and the return on their investments would be negligible [1]. To counter this problem, several UN agencies, including the World Health Organization, joined with AMREF and private foundations such as the Gates Foundation to support the development of a market for antimalarial drugs, thereby attracting the interest and cooperation of the drug industry. As a result, access to antimalarial drugs has increased, much to the benefit of the millions of children and adults affected by this scourge.

The problem of secure access to animal insulins, of course, affects far fewer people than the number who require antimalarial drugs. But we can learn from this successful strategy to involve the World Health Organization, governments and private foundations when addressing an important medical need. It is important to note that the International Diabetes Federation has acknowledged

[30] AMREF's website is accessible at http://www.amref.org/.

that animal insulins are an effective treatment for diabetes, that they are entirely acceptable and that unless there is a specific reason to convert patients from this treatment to 'human' insulin, patients should not be transferred [2].

The international campaign for affordable, safe animal insulin is just beginning. People who are actively involved will want to reach their goal quickly, especially because we sometimes feel that time is running against us. But as the first investigator to study the effects of 'human' insulin on blood sugar in the mid-1970s, I can offer a longer view. We need to build our campaign nationally and internationally and challenge the leading health authorities – including the World Health Organization – to take a progressive position on the need for animal insulin. This has already begun to happen and the momentum must now be moved forward. The honorable and ethical principles embraced by the co-discoverers of insulin including their commitment to sharing their discovery with all who need it should help guide us.

References

1 Sachs J, Kremer M: A cure for indifference. London Financial Times, May 5, 1999.
2 International Diabetes Federation: Position Statement: Animal, Human and Analogue Insulins, March 2005. http://www.idf.org/home/index.cfm?node = 1385. 1.3.2007.